THE
modern neurosis
HANDBOOK

Siggy

THE
modern neurosis
HANDBOOK

A Guide to Coping

Andrea Sarvady
Illustrated by Robin Zingone

LAUREL
GLEN

San Diego, California

Laurel Glen Publishing
An imprint of the Advantage Publishers Group
5880 Oberlin Drive, San Diego, CA 92121-4794
www.laurelglenbooks.com

All notations of errors or omissions should be addressed to Laurel
Glen Publishing, Editorial Department, at the above address. All other
correspondence (author inquiries, permissions, and rights) concerning
the content of this book should be addressed to Quirk Packaging, Inc.,
119 West 23rd Street, Suite 1001, New York, NY 10011.

Design by Lynne Yeamans

ISBN 1-59223-172-1
Library of Congress Cataloging-in-Publication Data
available upon request.

Printed in Singapore
1 2 3 4 5   08 07 06 05 04

acknowledgments *

FIRST AND FOREMOST, some kinda big fat trophy to Katherine Schulten for Best E-mail Forward Ever. Much gratitude for the eternal good humor and encouragement of Sharyn Rosart at Quirk Packaging. Thanks to the clever Betsy Beier, the visual delights of Robin Zingone and Lynne Yeamans, and the wonderful folks at Laurel Glen, who share our vision of an America free of crazy Americans. Info and inspiration came from Greg Changnon, Melissa Greene, Liza Hogan, Steve Klinge, Bob Orlowsky, and Barbara Petit— you kids put the "fun" in "dysfunction." Gratitude goes to Mom, Dad, and all the sibs for finally letting me drop the "sensitive" label (after observing years of insensitive behavior). Lastly, to Glen, Jocelyn, Rebecca, and Kate—you are the center of my disordered heart.

contents

introduction

IN AN ERA WHEN HALF THE POPULATION SEEMS TO BE ON PROZAC, when even dogs and cats are put in therapy, there are those who would argue, "Enough is enough! It's time to stop labeling every little emotional problem. People need to buck up, plow through, and get on with life."

Yes, there are those who would surely make that argument. We, however, are not those people. No, in fact, we would argue that the more you study our modern culture, the more you realize that there's scarcely a citizen alive not impaired by one neurosis or another. Our team of tireless researchers has uncovered a whole new group of disorders languishing on the waiting list of the bible of the mental health profession: the *Diagnostic Statistics Manual* (DSM). One may well wonder, "If these maladies are so detrimental to one's health, why aren't they recognized by the American Psychiatric Association and included in the latest DSM?"

The answer is plain and simple: time and money. It takes years for the APA to research, debate, and finally acknowledge the legitimacy of each new (or newly realized) psychological disorder. Yet few sufferers of Weekend Warrior Delusion can wait that long. And those afflicted with Weird Drink Addiction can ill afford the lobbyists needed to bring their affliction to light after spending half their salaries on cocktails that resemble lava lamps.

Until these disorders are given their due recognition by the psychiatric profession, something must be done to aid the afflicted. Although an obsession with e-mail may not be on the level of, say, amnesia, how can we deny the sufferer of this neurosis some relief? How can a compassionate society shower endless support on alcoholics yet turn away from those who continue to give their girlfriends ridiculous birthday gifts year after year, or, worse, who watch twenty or more hours of reality TV each week?

Fortunately, *The Modern Neurosis Handbook* is now readily available for those individuals who suffer from the little mental health problems that have emerged in today's fast-paced, self-absorbed, technology-ridden society. Afflictions that, although not life-threatening, can nevertheless wreak havoc on our sense of well-being. In terms that even a layperson can understand, the MNH describes a compendium of common afflictions, complete with checklists of symptoms, case studies, and easy-to-follow treatment plans developed by leading mental health professionals across the country.

The simple techniques presented here can be employed to cope with seemingly insurmountable problems and, ultimately, can effect great change in our lives. Whether you or a loved one suffer from a compulsion (E-mail Forwarding Compulsion, Tattoo Acquisition Compulsion), an obsession (Marriage Obsession, Celebrity-Watching Obsession), or a dating illness (Premature Relationship Dysfunction, "I Can Get That Hottie" Dysfunction),

MNH has a simple explanation of your malady and a treatment plan that's right for you. Unlike the DSM series, which addresses only psychological disorders afflicting a small percentage of the population, *The Modern Neurosis Handbook* identifies more common disorders that afflict nearly 100 percent of the population.

In a recent study, 300 randomly selected citizens were given a battery of tests to determine which, if any, modern neurosis they possess. The study showed that every subject exhibited signs of at least one of these neuroses and most struggled with five or more. Even more startling was the discovery that not one of these victims considered seeking professional help for these afflictions. Why? With no literature documenting their plight, they had no idea that they were dealing with a common — and treatable — disorder.

With this clear and compassionate guide, no longer will concerned citizens have to wonder if there's something wrong with them or if, like their loved ones often insist, it's "all in their head." *The Modern Neurosis Handbook* demonstrates to the reader that both things are true: There *is* something wrong with you. It *is* all in your head. Let us help fix it.

COMPULSION:

**A repetitive behavior
that serves no rational purpose**

large automobile acquisition
COMPULSION (A.K.A. SUV SYNDROME)

DO YOU HAVE LARGE AUTOMOBILE ACQUISITION COMPULSION?

A diagnosis should be based on the following criteria:

✳ You've convinced yourself that you need back-road traction for the treacherously uneven driveway in your company parking lot.

✳ You believe that for safety purposes you need to move above traffic at the eye level of a department store roof.

✳ You have had to enlarge the garage to accommodate your new vehicle. It is now bigger than your house.

✳ You require an intercom to communicate with passengers in the backseat.

✳ Your first car purchase was a modest Jeep, followed by a standard SUV, followed by an SUV in which passengers on the third bench are often riding in a different county than the driver.

background ✳

LAAC is becoming an increasingly common disorder, particularly in the United States, where citizens collectively suffer from "Bigger Is Better" syndrome. Onset of **LAAC** typically begins in the midtwenties for both men and women and lasts anywhere from ten to twenty years. Some individuals successfully transition to appropriate car purchasing through the help of therapeutic intervention. Others persist in their SUV obsessions or advance to **Prestige Automobile Buying Compulsion** as their economic situation improves.

treatment/recommendations *

LAAC is very difficult to treat after the vehicle has been purchased. However, prevention of future episodes is quite successful in individuals who attempt the following:

* **ASK YOURSELF: AM I A FIREFIGHTER?** If not, you might want to avoid purchasing an auto that requires hook-and-ladder skills to descend into the mall parking lot.

* **RECONSIDER THE AMOUNT OF SQUARE CUBIC FEET** needed to ferry yourself from place to place. You may conclude that although a car should be bigger than a bread box, it needn't be bigger than Belgium.

* **MINDFUL OF THE GAS-GUZZLING TENDENCIES OF THE SUV,** you tell others that you "care about the environment, but . . ." Take a good hard look at that "but." Do you really want to defend yourself against the angry glares of your children when they realize twenty years from now that it's your fault the hole in the ozone layer is now bigger than the entire continent?

what your car reveals about you

MIDSIZED COMPACT:	Trustworthy, dependable
WAGON:	Old-fashioned, or SUV-averse
MINIVAN:	Fertile
LUXURY SEDAN:	Rich, old money
LUXURY SUV:	Rich, new money
SPORTS CAR:	Feels twenty, looks forty, thinks looks twenty
CONVERTIBLE:	Unconcerned with hairstyle
TRUCK:	Can fix stuff when it breaks
LIMO:	Can afford new stuff when old stuff breaks
TINY, CUTE CAR:	Whimsical
HEARSE:	Really whimsical . . . or dead

e-mail forwarding
COMPULSION

DO YOU HAVE E-MAIL FORWARDING COMPULSION?

Siggy

A diagnosis should be based on the following criteria:

✳ You forward a minimum of ten nonessential e-mails a week to an enormous list of friends, colleagues, and casual acquaintances.

✳ You admit to confusion about what defines a "nonessential" e-mail.

✳ Your first thought upon reading "humorous" or "poignant" e-mails is "Who can I pass this along to?" Your usual answer: everyone in your address book.

✳ You've always enjoyed being part of chain letters, even before the advent of e-mail.

background ✳

A variety of disorders has arisen with the introduction of electronic mail. **E-mail Forwarding Compulsion** is distinct in its ability to negatively impact relationships (surpassed only by **Instant Messaging Addiction**). The forwarding compulsive is often unaware of the disorder until even spam mail operators refuse to send them messages, afraid of receiving missives even less desirable than their own.

treatment / recommendations *

Keep a log for one week noting the total number of e-mails you receive and how many you forward. Are the numbers the same? If yes, you may want to consider being more selective about whom you forward your e-mail to.

* **WALK YOURSELF THROUGH WHAT YOU WERE THINKING AND FEELING THE LAST TIME YOU COMPULSIVELY FORWARDED AN E-MAIL.**
Ask yourself, "What was in my mind when I sent the phlebotomist jokes? Do I know many people—or, for that matter, any people—who enjoy jokes about phlebotomists? Why might they appreciate receiving such an e-mail? Why not?"

* **NOTE IN YOUR LOG HOW MANY RESPONSES YOU RECEIVE TO YOUR FORWARDED E-MAILS** and pay careful attention to the subject titles of the responses. For example, "Stop Sending Me All This Crap!!!" indicates a respondent who does not share your appreciation of the forwarded e-mail. "Great New Jokes for Our Collection!" would be an example of a more positive response. Use subtle cues like these to weed out your audience.

* **TAKE A MINUTE TO ASSESS THE VALUES OF YOUR E-MAIL COMMUNITY,** then demonstrate proper restraint before damage is done. Consider this situation: You receive an e-mail entitled "An Inspirational Poem for My Women Friends." Just send it to all the women in your address book, right? Take a breath and reconsider. The women in your address book who collect angel memorabilia will surely revel in your thoughtfulness. Others may not be as appreciative.

* **REMIND YOURSELF EACH DAY** that while e-mail can be a wonderful way of bringing your community together, it will never match the gratitude you'll receive after buying the next round of drinks.

tattoo acquisition
COMPULSION

DO YOU HAVE TATTOO ACQUISITION COMPULSION?

Siggy

A diagnosis should be based on the following criteria:

* You have more than two tattoos, not counting that weird mole. (Get that checked, will you?)

* You claim to acquire tattoos out of inspiration rather than trendiness, as though you just saw a needle and thought, "Wow! I bet I could heat that up, put ink on it, and burn a rosebud on my ass!"

* One drunken night, you got excited because you thought you found a piece of tattoo-free skin, ripe for the needle. It turned out to be your tongue.

* Your friends think you're a total sellout for having the Charmin logo on your ankle. In reality, you showed up for your monthly tattooing session and just ran out of ideas. Then the tattoo guy went to take a leak and returned inspired.

background *

Tattoos were once a sign of lawless rebellion in this country. Now they are more likely to indicate that you work in marketing instead of finance. This has startled the true bohemians into getting more and more tattoos in a desperate attempt to keep their renegade status. At a certain point, **TAC** sets in and reasonable people turn themselves into Escher prints. The layperson might be flummoxed that anyone would put himself through repeated agony with so little to show for it. Yet consider the popularity of reality TV shows. (See **Reality TV Show Addiction**.)

treatment / recommendations *

If left unchecked, **Tattoo Acquisition Compulsion** can render you a permanent circus freak. Avoid this unfortunate outcome by attempting the following:

* **IF YOU FEEL YOUR TATTOOING IMPULSE IS OUT OF CONTROL,** try to analyze just which aspect of tattoo acquisition most appeals to you. Perhaps you're merely a sadomasochist who enjoys pain that leaves an irrevocable mark. In that case, you might want to consider walking in on your parents having sex instead.

did you know?

BODY ART HAS ENJOYED A LONG AND VARIED HISTORY. The first documented case of Tattoo Acquisition Compulsion in Western culture dates back to A.D. 790, when Viking warrior Ivor the Ferocious carved his moniker onto his bulging bicep with a spear. Pleased with the result, he immediately followed this up by having "Ivor ♥ Helga" emblazoned on his buttocks. Just four months later, the first recorded instance of tattoo removal occurred when Helga skipped town with Lars the Alluring.

* **THE TATTOO IMPULSE CAN BE KEPT IN CHECK** by steering clear of streets with more tattoo parlors than Starbucks and avoiding careers that encourage such adornment, e.g., performance art or holding up 7-Elevens.

* **IF YOU CAN'T SEEM TO CONTROL YOUR TATTOO ADDICTION,** at least make it work for you. Having trouble ending a difficult romance? Just tattoo "Amber 'n' Charlie 4 Ever" on your back. You're sure to be dumped the next day.

case history

* * *

Wes: The "Marked for Life" Man

FOR WES STONE IT ALL BEGAN with a girl. "Turquoise was something," he muses, pulling on a beer. He's proud of the fact that he burned her name onto his shoulder long before the tattoo craze hit its peak.

Though Wes and Turquoise barely lasted a calendar year, Wes and tattooing began a decade-long love affair. He turned "Turqoise" into a flower, then added a mermaid, and soon after a merman. "It was pretty cool to have a merman running across my butt," Wes mused, grabbing another beer, "but then it got kind of tired." To distract himself, Wes added the entire solar system to his arms and legs. "It'll be good for when I have kids," the forty-eight-year-old bachelor theorized. "They can do a lot of their homework by looking at naked old Dad."

Unfortunately, Wes is starting to regret his inky obsession. "I'm pretty sure I have that tattoo addiction problem," he admits, "but at least I've switched from transient relationships to more lasting stuff. Turquoise split for Reno with my rent money. But I don't see the Milky Way going anywhere."

inappropriately youthful clothing
COMPULSION

DO YOU HAVE INAPPROPRIATELY YOUTHFUL CLOTHING COMPULSION?

A diagnosis should be based on the following criteria:

* You agree that the adage "If you wore it the first time around, don't wear it the second" applies to so many people, yet, oddly enough, not to you.

* You wear a Speedo to the pool or beach and you are not (a) eighteen years old, (b) an Olympic swimmer, or (c) a German tourist.

* You get your fashion inspiration from edgy, downtown magazines— although that miniscule, smudgy type they use makes you grateful for your bifocals.

* Your son/daughter installed a lock on the closet door to stop you from borrowing clothes.

* You want your look to say, "I'm hot." Instead it says, "I'm having hot flashes."

background *

Inappropriately Youthful Clothing Compulsion (IYCC)
is one of the more challenging compulsions to treat. As with many
other psychological disorders, sufferers are not inclined to view themselves
as having a problem. Rather, they view themselves as fashion risk-takers, even
viewing the raised eyebrows and occasional laughter that follows in their wake as
a sign of their cutting-edge status.

treatment / recommendations *

Though **Inappropriately Youthful Clothing Compulsion** is, like all the narcissistic
disorders, resistant to treatment, the sufferer can often make a full recovery if forced
to face his or her denial. The following recommendations may help:

* **PULL OUT SOME OLD PHOTO ALBUMS.** See how your look has evolved over
  the years? Oh. That's right. Never mind.

* **CHECK OUT A BECKONING SHOP NEAR THE HIGH SCHOOL THAT YOUR
  CHILDREN ATTEND.** Are either tube tops or skateboards conspicuously
  displayed in the window? Is the store manager on your daughter's cheerleading
  squad? Are you tempted to go in? Walk on.

* **WHEN ADMIRING THE ETERNAL YOUTH OF MOVIE STARS,** note that
  they have a weapon far more powerful than trendy clothes or a workout regime.
  They have lighting.

* **BEAR IN MIND THAT THE SAYING** "You're as young as you feel!" is, like
  many sayings, complete crap.

JESSICA PHILLIPS LOVES CLOTHES and until recently she was under the impression that the mall was her oyster. This delusion was fostered in high school and college when friends would say, "Jessica, it's totally unfair. Everything looks good on you!"

Throughout her twenties, Jessica dressed like a club kid and basked in the many compliments she received. Yet after she turned thirty, things changed. "Jessica, you can really get away with that!" friends would exclaim, and she would bristle at the backhanded compliment. By the time she was forty, she began hearing, "Look at that outfit! Only Jessica!" followed by affectionate laughter.

At that point, the chastened clotheshorse galloped off to a therapist and learned that she had Inappropriately Youthful Clothing Compulsion (IYCC).

"I inherited the tendency from my mom," she admits now, recalling a mother who wore flowing hippie getups long after the revolution was over. With her therapist, Jessica learned to assess clothes not just for their intrinsic flair but for their suitability for a woman old enough to own property.

Treatment was very successful, largely due to Jessica's commitment and a savvy therapist, who had a cousin in retail. A card-carrying member of Banana Republic, Jessica now dresses like a stylish woman her age, and life is better. Well, most of the time. "I still miss my tube tops and low-rise jeans," she admits, "but I don't miss guys who think a great evening involves sharing a micro-wave burrito at the skate park."

permanently plugged-in
COMPULSION

DO YOU HAVE PERMANENTLY PLUGGED-IN COMPULSION?

A diagnosis should be based on the following criteria:

* You can't wait for someone to invent an underwater laptop so you can check your in-box while scuba diving.

* When a beeping sound fills your apartment, you madly dash from cell phone to Blackberry to laptop to try to figure out who's trying to reach you and on what.

* You can't resist opening every e-mail you receive the minute you receive it. Even the spam mail. Even the penis enlargement ads. Even though you're a lesbian.

* Ever since you bought your hands-free cell phone, you are often spotted wandering the streets alone, talking excitedly to no one. Even the guy in the aluminum foil hat crosses the street when he sees you coming.

background *

Permanently Plugged-In Compulsion (PPIC) affects more males than females, as do most of the **Standard Technological Disorders (STDs).** Women are often unfairly maligned as being overly talkative, but men rule the roost when it comes to communicating through gadgetry. Some historians trace this phenomenon back to early prehistoric dating rituals: while cavewomen prepared the fire for the buffalo, their dates would use the smoke to signal to the guys back home that they got lucky.

Individuals with **PPIC** become obsessed with using as many communication devices as possible, often two or three at a time, believing that constant access to these tools allows them to convey all the attributes of a desirable male: wealth, power, and the ability to thump vigorously on a tiny button.

treatment / recommendations *

Permanently Plugged-In Compulsion can best be alleviated by pulling the plug. Try the following:

* **MANY COMPULSIONS ARE KEPT IN CHECK** by the simple trick of snapping your wrist with a rubber band every time you're tempted to indulge. Yet this method might seem too low tech for the sufferer of **PPIC**. Instead, try text messaging yourself with a frowny-face icon.

* **HAND YOUR ROOMMATE A BAG WITH ALL YOUR BATTERIES IN IT,** saying, "No matter how hard I beg, don't give these back to me." Then lock yourself in the closet until the shakes go away.

* **MAKE AMENDS TO ALL THE PEOPLE YOU'VE IGNORED OR ABUSED DURING YOUR LONG PLUGGED-IN OBSESSION.** Explain to your great-grandmother that it was the *disease* talking when you called her a moron because she didn't know how to send an e-mail.

* **IF YOU CHOOSE TO LIVE WITH PPIC, THAT'S FINE.** Just know that it may be challenging to find a life partner who doesn't mind if you sell stocks during sex.

case history

✳ ✳ ✳

Grant: The Technology Junkie

GRANT HOGAN LOVED THE FACT THAT he was born in an era in which he could be contacted at any minute of the day. He was amazed that some fellow citizens refused to take advantage of this technological boon.

"I would call people," he'd marvel, "and *they wouldn't answer the phone.* Isn't that unbelievable? Of course, everyone screens now and then, but they wouldn't even check to see who it was. I'd confront them later and they'd just give me some lame excuse like 'Our kitchen was on fire.' I mean, *really.* How long does it take to pick up the phone?"

Grant answered the phone, grabbed a fax, checked the Blackberry, sent e-mail, and otherwise used electronic communication devices at all times. Friends complained that they had better luck getting his attention on cell phones than in person. His family argued that even a *top-ranked* event coordinator should turn off the beeper during his son's birth.

It was then that Grant finally realized that he had a PPIC. Through months of work at the Institute for Human Connection, Grant relearned to communicate with others using nothing more than his natural (analog) voice and a friendly expression. He is now capable of going more than an hour without using any technological devices, and his son is reaping the benefits.

"Pixel and I are really building a relationship," Grant says proudly of his six-month-old son, "and I can't wait to show him how to build a Web site—I mean, a block tower. Yeah, that's it."

personal disclosures to strangers
COMPULSION

DO YOU HAVE PERSONAL DISCLOSURES TO STRANGERS COMPULSION?

Siggy

A diagnosis should be based on the following criteria:

* You view every stranger as a friend that you haven't met. No, more like a close family member.

* Charades is fun, but nothing gets a party going like playing "My Most Humiliating Sexual Experience."

* Sure, everyone finds it difficult to talk at the dentist's, what with all that junk they stick in your mouth. You figure they're on a tight schedule, because they stuff your mouth while you're still in the waiting room.

* Here's something you hear a lot: "Wow. That must have been really hard for you . . . Taxi!"

* You feel so much closer to people after you tell them how you overcame your wire-hanger fetish. Now you can *finally* have an honest relationship with your dry cleaner.

background *

Personal Disclosures to Strangers Compulsion (PDTSC) began to flourish in the early 1970s, when the popularity of self-help books and workshops began to take off. From confessional memoirists to talk show exhibitionists, the "Me Generation" eventually morphed into the "Cry with Me" generation. While the healthy individual has a well-developed sense of privacy and personal space, many people—perhaps fearful of being considered repressed—take the healthy impulse of "sharing" to bizarre extremes.

personal disclosures by the numbers

Number of people this year who explained
that they wrote their memoirs "to help people":

912

Number of people actually helped:

912

Percentage of people who want to hear about your unsettling desires:

8

Percentage if you're a gorgeous female:

84

Percentage if you're Howard Stern:

98

Appropriate age to tell parent of sexual history/drug usage:

50

Appropriate age to tell child of sexual history/drug usage:

150

treatment / recommendations *

If you are afflicted with **PDTSC** it would be wise for you to realize that there is nothing wrong with disclosing highly personal information to a complete stranger provided that it is done within the "fifty-minute hour" and that your check is good. You should also consider the following self-healing treatments:

* **THE NEXT TIME YOU ANNOUNCE TO A CROWD,** "Sometimes I feel like smearing tuna casserole all over my naked body," see how many heads nod in agreement, how many choruses of "Me too!" ring in your ears. None, right? You've just taken the first step on the road to recovery.

* **IT MAY BE HELPFUL TO USE A DELAY TACTIC** to curb this compulsion. The next time you're tempted to blurt out something personal, try biting your arm instead. It may hurt, but it's better than having the rest of the firehouse know you're addicted to *Style Court*.

* **REMIND YOURSELF** that there are many respectable ways to grab a few minutes of national attention. Detailing your impure thoughts involving hamsters to millions of Americans and a fatuous talk show host is not one of them.

* **IT'S TRUE THAT INTIMATE CONFESSIONS HELP PEOPLE GROW CLOSER.** But take care to avoid using this as a rationalization for your behavior. It is intimate to share secrets with that special someone; it is promiscuous to share them with New Jersey.

PHOBIA:

Fear of a situation or object

family reunion
PHOBIA

background ✳

Due to the boundary issues that beset all families, reunions are intrinsically stressful and can cause even the healthiest person to fill with dread. Explore the following: Does anticipation of attending a reunion make my life unmanageable? Is my identity shaken to the core in the presence of my family? And, perhaps most important, now that I've stumbled upon my aunts naked in the hot tub, can someone please burn out my eyes?

treatment/recommendations *

This common phobia is perhaps most easily eradicated by eradicating your family. Yet **Life in Prison Phobia** would simply take its place. A gentler solution might be the following:

* **ROLE PLAYING CAN BE AN EFFECTIVE TECHNIQUE** for alleviating a phobia. In other words, rehearse methods for dealing with your family by meeting with people who scare you and hitting them up for money.

* **REMEMBER: BABY STEPS.** You don't have to come out at this reunion, no matter what your gay support group says. (Besides, who do you think you're fooling? Maybe your uncle with **Ice-Dancing Mania,** but he's not even on to himself yet.)

* **EVERY TIME A RELATIVE SAYS SOMETHING NASTY TO YOU,** write it down in a notebook. Now imagine turning that notebook into a best-selling memoir. Now imagine a real cutie in the front row at your book signing thinking, "I've just got to sleep with the valiant soul who went through all that."

* **NOTE:** Perhaps the family reunion is a sports-filled weekend in Colorado and you haven't got an athletic bone in your body. Or maybe your extended family enjoys spending weekends together in Manhattan, but you panic at the sight of buildings higher than three stories. This doesn't mean you have a phobia; it means you were adopted. Go find your real family.

case history

✳ ✳ ✳

Gary and Rachel: Twin Phobics

TWINS GARY AND RACHEL HIRSCH share many traits, yet they differ greatly in their approach to family functions. Rachel loves mingling with a room full of relatives; Gary would rather hang himself than endure one more conversation about why a nice guy like him hasn't settled down yet.

"I sort of see the whole Hirsch experience as a movie," explains Rachel, a documentary filmmaker, "but Gary lacks that distance."

It was this insight that inspired their mutual therapist to suggest that they actually turn the next family gathering into a documentary film. Cousin Amy's wedding became *Hirsch Love*. The film may not have won any honors at Cannes, but Gary is thankful he can now go home for the holidays without developing hives.

geographical
PHOBIA

DO YOU HAVE A GEOGRAPHICAL PHOBIA?

A diagnosis should be based on the following criteria:

TYPE A: Fear of the Coasts

* Friends keep leaving for Los Angeles to make it in "the industry." They are never heard from again. You are forced to conclude that "the industry" is some kind of maximum-security prison.

* Everyone out west seems too mellow. Everyone back east seems too angry. You choose to live in North Dakota.

* Psych wards are filled with people wandering around in weird clothes who think they're God's gift to the world. But so are San Francisco and Miami.

* Some people look out at the ocean and envision the sublime beauty of the infinite. You see the *Titanic* going under.

* Sure, you miss the sophisticated nightlife you'd find in L.A. or New York: the avant-garde dance troupes, the visiting operas from Düsseldorf . . . Oh, who are we kidding? You'd take a Budweiser and a Vin Diesel flick over that stuff any day of the week.

TYPE B: Fear of the Vast Middle

✴ Sushi! Sushi! You can't survive more than three days without fresh sushi!

✴ There's nothing like endless blue skies stretching overhead to force one to contemplate one's own insignificance in the larger scheme of life. Like *that's* something you want to do.

✴ A drive through the country sounds charming. Yet you're terrified that an inopportune car breakdown will force you to participate in a barn raising, with men who look nothing like Harrison Ford in *Witness*.

✴ After finding out that this year's conference is in Omaha, you console yourself with visions of those famous steaks. Then you remember that you're a vegan.

background ✳

With the rise in low-cost air travel, geographical phobias have increased exponentially as Americans run out of excuses to avoid weddings in Wyoming and conventions in Manhattan. To properly analyze this twin phobia, media bias must be taken into account. Although it would seem to many that **Fear of the Vast Middle** far exceeds **Fear of the Coasts,** this is only because coastal people write all the TV shows.

treatment / recommendations ✳

Geographical Phobias are relatively harmless. Yet why leave any psychological malady untreated? Many find the following techniques beneficial:

✳ **GRAB A FEW PHOBIC FRIENDS** and drive through the part of the United States you find most upsetting. Ignore the bad fashions and strange food and focus on what really matters: these people may be as annoying as your worst relatives, but at least you get to whiz by them at seventy miles per hour.

✳ **EMBRACING ALL OF AMERICA TAKES PRACTICE** for the geographical phobic. Try to remember that with the exception of how we dress, what we eat, how we worship, how we vote, what we think, what matters most to us, and who we can stand to be around for more than five minutes, all Americans are pretty much the same.

✳ **FOR A "COLD TURKEY" APPROACH TO YOUR PHOBIA,** put on a blindfold, throw a thumbtack across the room at a map, and go live wherever the thumbtack lands. As you'll be throwing from across the room, the tack will simply hit the wall and land on your own floor. Congratulations! Another phobia successfully overcome.

TWENTY-SEVEN-YEAR-OLD LISETTE DAHL was the perfect New Yorker. You'd never catch her on the wrong subway train or living in the wrong part of the wrong borough. She never missed an A-list party, an edgy gallery opening, or a provocative reading.

Then, tragedy struck. She lost her job, the economy plummeted, and marketing jobs became as scarce as edamame in Missouri. To her horror, the only job offer she got was in Cleveland, Ohio. With college loans to pay and a serious shoe-shopping habit, she had no choice but to take the job.

Upon arriving in Cleveland, Lisette immediately sought help for her Geographical Phobia. Her lifestyle coach recommended an arty neighborhood and a few restaurants, and before long Lisette was actually enjoying herself. She found her favorite brand of soy milk at a fraction of the cost she paid in SoHo, and she discovered a salon that gave respectable pedicures.

"There are some interesting people in Ohio," she now admits with wonder. "I have a group of friends who like the same music and books that I do. What's more, they have healthy relationships, enjoy spending time with their parents, and send thank-you notes after dinner parties."

Still, Lisette has no plans to spend the rest of her life in Cleveland. For this reason, she's troubled by her recent relationship with Noah, a guy so great she can't imagine leaving him behind when the job market picks up. "He's not quite screwed up enough for New York," she admits, "but I'll work on that. That's what love is all about, right?"

signs of aging
PHOBIA (A.K.A. CHER SYNDROME)

DO YOU HAVE SIGNS OF AGING PHOBIA?

A diagnosis should be based on the following criteria:

∗ You laugh along with everyone else at a good Botox joke. That is, you attempt to laugh.

∗ Your highlights cost more than your car payments.

∗ Discovering that sunglasses are the perfect inexpensive antidote to crow's feet, you've taking to wearing them 24/7. Boy Scouts often volunteer to guide you across the street at intersections.

∗ Looking young is important to you, but it's not like it's a full-time job. Well, yes, it is.

background ∗

Closely related to **Inappropriately Youthful Clothing Compulsion, Signs of Aging Phobia (SOAP)** soared dramatically with the advent of age-defying medical treatments. More than ever, it strikes many as unseemly to wear the marks of a well-traveled life. Yet a well-traveled life is exactly what makes us interesting to others. Thus, for sufferers of SOAP, the motto is "Be yourself . . . but look like a wax statue of yourself."

treatment/recommendations ✳

Once you've decided that looking embalmed is worse than looking old, try the following:

✳ **MAKE FRIENDS WITH YOUR ENCROACHING WRINKLES.**
Give them names. Try outlining them with permanent marker as a show of "wrinkle pride."

✳ **REALITY CHECK NO. 1:** Those waiters don't really believe that you and your daughter are sisters. They believe that good tips result from their ability to lie convincingly.

✳ **REALITY CHECK NO. 2:** A rakish, disheveled hairstyle looks sexy on a young man. On an older man, it looks like you stumbled aimlessly out of assisted living.

✳ **WANT TO FEEL YOUNG?** It's all relative. Stop watching MTV, start watching *The Golden Girls*.

✳ **THE NEXT TIME YOU'RE RUSHING TO "GET SOME WORK DONE,"** ask yourself: Who am I really doing this for? Some gorgeous stud I met at a club who thinks I'm in my twenties? Some aging billionaire who lavishes luxuries on women he thinks are half his age? If either case applies, go right ahead.

home renovation
PHOBIA

DO YOU HAVE HOME RENOVATION PHOBIA?

A diagnosis should be based on the following criteria:

✳ You think *This Old House* is a horror show.

✳ Your avocado-and-gold '60s kitchen is all the envy of your friends. Or so they say.

✳ You buy an ancient farmhouse and won't renovate it, despite the lack of indoor plumbing—or a roof.

✳ Although a renovation would work wonders on your place, you can't bear the thought of moving in with your father and his slobbering mastiff while the work is being done.

background ✳

Home renovation is on the rise, with many folks flocking to the safety of the nest in response to frightening world events. Yet phobics remain unconvinced that the best antidote to terrorism and disease is a newly tiled powder room. Their life is a constant existential torment, filled with questions like: How does one define sanctuary? Do we build for ourselves or for the next generation? Would it kill the painters to share some of their drugs?

home renovation by the numbers

How much time the average renovation is presumed to take:

2 months

How long it actually takes:

6 years

Average cost of medium-sized renovation:

$50,000

Amount of that spent on double lattes for crew:

$5,000

Most popular type of renovation:

gourmet kitchen

What most homeowners wished they'd settled for:

fire pit

Percentage of homeowners who say it was worth it:

100%

Percentage under heavy medication at the time:

100%

treatment/recommendations *

Home Renovation Phobia is a normal response to an untenable situation. Nonetheless, treatment can reduce anxiety. Consider the following:

* **SOMETIMES WHAT APPEARS TO BE HOME RENOVATION PHOBIA** is really masking other home-related fears. When your architect draws up a blueprint, make sure he or she includes not only a safe room, but also a secret escape hatch that leads down to the river, where someone will be waiting with the getaway chopper.

* **PEOPLE WILL TELL YOU THAT IT IS A GOOD IDEA TO MOVE OUT WHILE RENOVATING.** It is more than a good idea. It is suicide prevention.

* **IN THE END, SOME PHOBIAS ARE ONLY ERADICATED BY "GOING FOR IT."** So, at a certain point you just have to chuck your inhibitions, tell yourself that it will be worth it in the end and plunge into the experience. In other words, sleep with the contractor.

* **SOMETIMES STARTING SMALL EASES THE FEAR** of changing your home environment. Begin by swapping out old pictures of your family with more recent photos. Then try throwing out one family member and bringing in a new one.

OBSESSION:

An idea or impulse that is recurrent, persistent, and senseless

marriage
OBSESSION

DO YOU HAVE MARRIAGE OBSESSION?

A diagnosis should be based on the following criteria:

TYPE A: Marriage Attainment

* You're so desperate to get married that you're willing to have the wedding at a venue that's more convenient for him—even though prison catering sucks.

* Your latest hunt for a wife involves inviting attractive women to join you in a rented mansion while you throw them out one by one, finally allowing a television audience to choose your bride. (See also: **Reality Television Show Addiction.**)

* You've had Vera Wang on speed dial for years—just in case.

* Those bridal magazines are awesome, but they never have articles that teach you how to *make* the guy marry you.

TYPE B: Marriage Avoidance

✷ Marriage is a great idea, but not until you finish your postdoctoral work. Of course, this may take a while, since you just received your GED.

✷ You're a lesbian. What avoidance?

✷ It's not the idea of marriage that bothers you, it's that stupid public ceremony. The fancy clothes, the cheesy vows, the bad music. Oh, and the monogamy.

✷ Why do people have to *own* each other? Wouldn't it be more liberating for people to just have really great sex and then, I don't know, make dinner?

background *

With the advent of feminism and other sorts of liberation, it's a wonder that marriage has the same hold on society it has had since ancient times. Some attribute this obsession to our love/hate relationship with ice sculptures. Others theorize that your type of **Marriage Obsession** can best be determined by whether you respond with envy or revulsion to this sentence: "Honey, you've got a little . . . on your lip there . . . no, over a little. There. You got it."

treatment / recommendations *

Marriage Obsession can strike in different ways at different times in your life. If you've made a commitment to healing yourself, recite the following:

* **FRANTIC TO GET MARRIED?** Start spending time with an unhappily married couple. Terrified of marriage? Enjoy the company of a blissful, loving couple. None of this will change your mind, of course, but you'll have fun mocking both couples with your friends.

* **WHETHER OR NOT YOU GET MARRIED IS STRICTLY YOUR BUSINESS.** Yet bear in mind that if you're a truly revolting human being, you'll do society a kindness by finding someone equally revolting and taking yourself off the market.

* **HOW SMART OF YOU TO PLAN A LONG ENGAGEMENT!** Just remember: if he's putting off marriage until he finishes medical school, he's practical. If he's putting off marriage until he finds an apartment with the right feng shui for his Maltese terrier, he's gay.

* **A MARRIAGE IS AS UNIQUE AS A FOOTPRINT.** Realize that footprints change over time, with toenail-clipping procedures becoming more unbearable with each passing year, until you're finally ready to explode in disgust and hatred toward your revolting, toenail-clipping life partner. Isn't that inspiring?

health regimen discussion OBSESSION

DO YOU HAVE HEALTH REGIMEN DISCUSSION OBSESSION?

A diagnosis should be based on the following criteria:

✻ When you walk into the gym, everyone suddenly slams on their headphones and blasts loud music. Even your personal trainer.

✻ You've had to drop some friends who became boring and stuck in their own little world. A shame, considering all the new butt exercises there are to talk about.

✻ You find yourself jealous when your friend discusses her baby—not because you want kids, but because little Brandon sounds like just the twelve-pound weight you've been looking for.

✻ You've started sleeping with your herbalist. He's fifty years older than you and smells a little like dry rot—but does he know enemas!

✻ You had to quit your job because it became a downer to be surrounded by such dumpy, serious people who took no interest in your newfound love of kickboxing. Oh well. Who wanted to work at the White House anyway?

background *

Individuals with **Health Regimen Discussion Obsession (HRDO)** often have jobs in the diet or fitness industry, so a certain degree of shoptalk is normal. However, exaggerated levels of discussion may occur when these individuals are under stress or are forced to cope with a trauma (a death in the family, a serious accident, a two-pound weight gain). Sufferers of **HRDO** irritate employers, lose romantic partners, and alienate friends with endless tales of their health habits. The good news is they still look hot.

treatment/recommendations *

Health Regimen Discussion Obsession can be overcome if sufferers simply apply the same diligence to recovery that they do to watching their carb intake. Consider the following:

* **TAKE OUT A NOTEBOOK AND RECORD** every instance when you feel the urge to talk about your health regimen. For organizational effectiveness, get a fresh start—don't use your calorie counting notebook, your workout notebook, your vitamin intake notebook, or your heart rate notebook.

* **CHANGE IS DIFFICULT; START SLOW.** Early conversations might have to incorporate your health regimen with other topics. When leaving yoga class, try asking a fellow student: "How do you think global warming would be affected by my switching from Iyengar to Bikram?"

* **IT'S NOT THAT YOUR RELATIVES DON'T WANT TO LEARN** all about your new potato diet. It's just that they learn more by your actions than your words. So, keep chewing those potatoes. That's it. No—don't talk. Just keep chewing.

* **AS YOU ATTEMPT TO STRENGTHEN STRAINED RELATIONSHIPS,** try phone calls rather than in-person visits. That way, when you say, "How are you feeling today?" friends don't have to know that you're talking to your triceps.

TWENTY-SIX-YEAR-OLD KRISTIN ANDERSON was thrilled when she lost twenty-four pounds and six inches on her new health regimen. "I felt so great!" she recalls. "It seemed selfish not to share my discoveries with friends." Kristin's friends were clamoring to know how she did it, and she was eager to tell them. She'd point out healthy menu choices and encourage everybody to try the Pilates class at the gym. "I loved her new energy," one friend recalls. "At first, it was great."

What became less great as time wore on was Kristin's growing obsession with her low-carb, high-intensity lifestyle. Whenever she got together with her friends, she would attempt to steer the conversation to healthy living. "What a bummer," they recall her saying upon hearing of a friend's dad's gallstones. "*Somebody* didn't eat his green leafy veggies!"

Her book group was not really impressed by her critique of *The Hunchback of Notre Dame*: "That dude so did not stretch before working out." For her boyfriend, Craig, that was the last straw. Embarrassed by his girlfriend's obsession, Craig introduced Kristin to his aunt, a therapist specializing in treating people whose hobbies have made them incredibly uninteresting.

By applying art therapy, guided imagery, and duct tape over her mouth at parties, Kristin learned to start viewing her health regimen as just one component of her multifaceted personality. "I'm so much more well rounded now," she admits. "Craig and I didn't work out, which was sad, but I'm meeting lots of new guys who seem to think I'm really interesting. Especially when I show them my stomach muscles."

celebrity-watching
OBSESSION

background *

Back in the days of the studio system, carefully choreographed glimpses into the stars' "real lives" allowed us to feel that we were getting the real scoop on the wonderful marriage of Richard Burton and Elizabeth Taylor and the fabulous parenting skills of Joan Crawford. As the studios lost their singular hold on actors, stars became far less discriminating about what they said in interviews and how they acted in public. Suddenly, the unwashed masses found it plausible to enroll in a yoga class with an actor or engage in an e-mail debate with a beloved rock star. For this reason, **CWO** has become a nationwide epidemic (homeschoolers and that environmentalist who sat in a tree for two years are exempt).

treatment / recommendations *

Celebrity-Watching Obsession can best be cured by getting a life. If you find that an unrealistic goal, consider the following:

* **WHEN DETERMINING THE DEGREE OF YOUR DYSFUNCTION,** ask yourself to what extent **CWO** has taken over your decision-making processes. Did you once ask for a supermodel's autograph at a Starbucks? Not a problem. Did you then purchase that Starbucks in case she came in again? More of an issue.

* **MANY SUFFERERS FIND THAT LEARNING ABOUT THE GREAT LEADERS** in history is an antidote to obsessing about entertainers. Granted, Mahatma Gandhi never made a guest appearance on *Will & Grace*, but he still did a few cool things in his day.

* **THERAPY HAS ENABLED MANY INDIVIDUALS** stricken with **CWO** to realize how they have used their obsession as a distraction from the problems in their own lives. In other words, if you've been fired from your job, dumped by your spouse, and the El Camino you've been sleeping in for the past three weeks was repossessed, perhaps Liza Minnelli's dog's spa treatments shouldn't be your greatest concern.

* **IT IS UNWISE TO MISTAKE CELEBRITY ENDORSEMENTS FOR EXPERT ADVICE.** That star is not thin because of the diet she's encouraging you to try. That star is thin because eating is expressly forbidden in her movie contract.

media-influenced health OBSESSION

DO YOU HAVE MEDIA-INFLUENCED HEALTH OBSESSION?

Siggy

A diagnosis should be based on the following criteria:

✳ You scan the paper every morning to see what's wrong with you since yesterday afternoon.

✳ You hear about a new disease sweeping through Thailand and think, "Oh, no! I ate at Thai Kitchen just last week!"

✳ The Center for Disease Control is number one on your speed dial list. It's also number two, number three, number four . . .

✳ A big news story on Dutch elm disease keeps you up at night. You neglect to consider that you are neither Dutch nor an elm.

background ✳

Hypochondria is nothing new, but never before have we had the opportunity to learn all about a new disease within moments of its first appearance. The minute two people who may have both been in the same place at the same time come down with similar symptoms, their plight is given a name, a celebrity spokesperson, and a walk-a-thon. **Media-Influenced Health Obsession** has emerged among the ranks of the fashionable citizens of our society—those who live by the trends to such a degree that they can only imagine dying by a trend as well.

treatment/recommendations *

Sick of feeling sick? Try this Rx:

* **THE MINUTE THE NEWS TURNS TO HEALTH COVERAGE,**
switch channels and watch something more uplifting. You are unlikely to
have the latest infectious disease, but you just might learn to celebrate life from
7th Heaven reruns. Or not.

* **FIND A DOCTOR YOU REALLY TRUST,** the
kind who truly feels that "there are no stupid
questions." Then, ask away: Can I get
hamster pox from a toilet seat? Are
mad cows really mad, or just slightly
disgruntled? We all know Superman is
fake, but what about kryptonite?

* **WHEN YOU HEAR THAT YOU
CAN REDUCE YOUR ODDS OF
DEATH** by disease by
avoiding exotic locales,
food, and people,
you resolve to move
to a fully stocked
gated community,
where you'll only risk
dying of boredom.

first baby
OBSESSION

DO YOU HAVE FIRST BABY OBSESSION?

A diagnosis should be based on the following criteria:

✻ You had always planned to wait three months before telling people that you were pregnant, "just in case." Instead, you put five people on a conference call while awaiting the results of your home pregnancy test.

✻ Always a casual decorator, you now find yourself drawn to the most elaborate baby furnishings, with wall borders that match crib sheets that match diaper pail liners.

✻ You spend hours each evening discussing the parenting lapses of friends (too much television, not enough fresh fruit, only one language spoken in the home . . .). Your judgments are sound and reasonable; after all, there are no greater experts on parenting than people about to have their first child.

✻ Sure, everybody talks about the "second coming." You're the first couple to actually *do* something about it.

background ✻

First Baby Obsession is hardly a new disorder. Total strangers will treat a pregnant woman's stomach like it's a magic lamp. Colleagues will ask, "When's the due date?" approximately twice a day until you go on maternity leave four months early just to stay sane. The only known cure for **First Baby Obsession** is pregnancy with a second baby, which people—particularly the first baby—are less excited about.

treatment/recommendations *

Your first pregnancy is a special time. At least for you, that is.
Others might be busy searching for world peace or trying to hook up.
To stop yourself from becoming a crazed bore, try the following:

* **BEGIN BY ACKNOWLEDGING** that if you *were* the first person on the
  planet to have a baby, then there would be no one to administer the epidural.

* **YOU MAY BE TEMPTED TO BUY EVERYTHING** under the sun for a baby as
  gorgeous as yours. As a cost-saving measure, try to see your baby through the eyes
  of a single person: as a squirmy little alien who steals women's breasts.

* **ONCE THE BABY ARRIVES,** it is difficult to imagine being away from your
  child. Yet it's very important for the health of your relationship to spend time
  alone with your spouse without the baby. After the newborn has settled into a
  routine, invite a grandparent or trusted friend to stop by one afternoon to hold
  the baby. Then leave for Europe.

did you know?

A STUDY OF EXPECTING COUPLES found that an overwhelming percentage of child rearers change identities along with diapers. The study, which followed 312 adults through pregnancy, labor, and early childhood, revealed that in every single case both members of the couple underwent a renaming process. "Mom" and "Mama" were found to be overwhelming female favorites; men were commonly christened "Daddy," "Dada," and "It's *Your* Turn, Buddy."

catalog-flipping
OBSESSION

A diagnosis should be based on the following criteria:

✶ At current count, 120 catalogs arrive at your home on a weekly basis—and you are physically unable to toss any of them without at least a cursory glance.

✶ You eagerly await the arrival of this week's gourmet cooking utensil catalog and read it greedily as you shovel in your nightly carton of cheap takeout food.

✶ You buy a complete outfit in "wheatflower heather" and find yourself positively shocked when it turns out to be simply beige.

✶ You particularly enjoy the nostalgia-drenched catalogs that take us back to our glorious childhoods . . . Of course, no one actually *had* such a childhood, but that doesn't keep you from maxing out all your credit cards to get it now.

✶ You make sure to always have a large stack of catalogs waiting for your perusal in the bathroom, and the bedroom, and your office drawer, and the car, and tucked in your favorite church pew.

✶ Your friends mock your catalog collection, but they don't understand that sometimes you need to see an item to realize that you need it. Now if only someone could build a fireplace in your studio apartment to go with your new Hand-Forged Iron Fire-Tending Set.

case history

Vanessa: Flipping Out

VANESSA SPEARS KNEW SHE HAD A PROBLEM the day the mail didn't come. A large snowstorm prevented her carrier from delivering that day; the roads were just too dangerous. "I literally had the shakes," she recalls. "I mean, I had been conditioned to expect that every day at four a batch of new catalogs would pour down the slot. There's nothing better than an afternoon cup of tea and a stack of catalogs. Nothing. Well, maybe my husband's surviving that car accident last year, but that's it."

She catches herself. "I mean, this is the kind of thing I used to think. Then I got help." When Vanessa's savings had all gone to impulse purchases of bathroom fixtures that weren't needed or patio furniture that wouldn't fit on her condo balcony, she turned to the Society to Combat Retail Pornography. There, a trained clinician convinced her that sleek ads detailing an impossibly chic life were no substitute for real living.

It's been six months since Vanessa's therapy and she's slipped up only once. "I canceled all the catalogs, but a neighbor left one here," she confesses. "For one blissful hour I pored over the descriptions and stroked every glamorous photo. It was heaven. I hadn't been that happy since my husband finished rehab. No, since my four-hundred-thread-count sheets arrived from Maine last fall. Wait, no, definitely the rehab."

background *

The ease of telephone and e-mail communication—not to mention rampant laziness—has made personal mail almost completely a thing of the past. Bills and catalogs now clog the nation's mailboxes. In comparison to bills, catalogs seem friendlier and more inviting. Their attractive pictures and tempting descriptions seem to promise consumers the chance to purchase happiness, a new life, or at least a set of personalized branding irons. **Catalog-Flipping Obsession** develops in people starved for human contact, who haven't yet realized that catalogs are merely bills that haven't arrived yet.

treatment / recommendations *

Those who relieve themselves of this obsession report both economic and psychological benefits. Try the following:

* **CATALOG FLIPPING IS A TOUGH HABIT TO BREAK** and "cold turkey" is sometimes the only effective approach. Throw out every catalog that comes into your home. You'll still receive dozens of catalogs at work, of course, but at least you've reduced your mindless reading to those hours when you're on the clock.

* **GO THROUGH EACH OF YOUR CATALOGS** asking yourself, "Would I be happier if I owned this? Would life be better if I purchased this?" Note that the honest answer is always "no"—unless you're looking at the chocolate catalogs.

* **EVERY YEAR CATALOG FLIPPERS THINK THAT THEY CAN COMBAT THE INSANITY** of Christmas and Hanukkah by doing all their shopping by mail. Yet, every year, despite hours of reading and planning, certain items still require a trip to the mall. Look at it this way: Mary gave birth in a manger, and Judas Maccabee fought for years to win back a lousy oil lamp. God wants you to suffer, too.

DELUSION:

A belief regarding oneself or the world
that a person holds despite
overwhelming evidence to the contrary

PART IV **delusions**

arrogant road-owner DELUSION

DO YOU HAVE ARROGANT ROAD-OWNER DELUSION?

Siggy

A diagnosis should be based on the following criteria:

* You often get arrested for speeding—on the autobahn.

* You think signaling is for wusses.

* You honk at people only if there's a good reason. Like they're about to hit you. Or they aren't moving at a light. Or you don't like their bumper sticker. Or they're ugly.

* Speaking of bumper stickers, you have a lot of them, because people should know just who they're dealing with. After all, your kid is an honor student, your guy won the election, and you've seen "Rock City." Out of the way, losers!

background *

Arrogant Road-Owner Delusion (AROD) affects far more males than females; women are more likely to forget that they're *on* the road than think they own it. Thus, the morning commute often begins with men screaming at their wives to stop putting on makeup and get out of the bathroom, so they can hit the road and get stuck behind more women putting on makeup. Men afflicted with **AROD** are quick to conclude that this is some massive female conspiracy to drive them insane and keep them from bulleting down the highway at the speed of light. Not a bad theory.

treatment/recommendations ✳

Nobody wants to be hated—even by strangers they'll never see again.
Curb your road-warrior tendencies with these techniques:

✳ **DELUSIONS ARE BEST COMBATED WITH DOSES OF REALITY.** The next
time you go to Daytona, ask yourself: Am I down there on the track? No? Then
why do I drive 190 miles an hour and expect a pit crew to replace my tires when
they explode?

✳ **THOSE AFFLICTED WITH AROD** often have difficulty remembering that other
vehicles are filled with human beings. On your next drive, take a good look at your
fellow travelers. Sure, you have your differences. Yet you share the same dream of
returning home from errands in a car rather than a body bag.

✳ **IF YOU SIMPLY CAN'T CONTROL YOUR ROAD-OWNER TENDENCIES,** turn
the driving over to someone else and ride where no one will be bothered by your
maniacal behavior—the trunk.

arrogant road-owner
by the numbers

Speed at which Arrogant Road-Owners usually drive on highways:

85 mph

On city streets:

80 mph

In church parking lots:

70 mph

Most frequent excuse for speeding:

"i was in a hurry."

Most common place they were in a hurry to get to:

mcdonald's

Percent of ugly men able to talk their way out of a ticket:

14%

Percent of pretty women able to do the same:

92%

Change in this number since women joined the highway patrol:

0%

"i'm parenting a special child"
DELUSION

DO YOU HAVE "I'M PARENTING A SPECIAL CHILD" DELUSION?

Siggy

A diagnosis should be based on the following criteria:

* You knew from that first ultrasound picture what a winning fetus you had. That aristocratic profile, the sophisticated slouch—even the umbilical cord had a certain je ne sais quoi.

* Sure, your Arielle has trouble getting along with others. She's just "spirited." Didn't Einstein set all his playmates on fire, too? Or was it Mozart?

* Your child's gifts are so numerous. Last week she handled that chocolate pudding like an expressionist painter. And just today, she pulled apart her chicken nugget like a surgeon. That's it! She'll be an artist-slash-surgeon!

* You've noticed that the other parents at your workplace don't seem to talk about their children as much as you do. You assume it's because there's just not that much to tell.

background *

It's a biological imperative to be smitten with your offspring; such blind adoration enables the species to perpetuate. Yet those stricken with **"I'm Parenting a Special Child" Delusion (IPASCD)** insist that their particular species representative has all the makings of the next Dalai Lama. Ironically, offspring of those afflicted with **IPASCD** are usually not spectacular in the slightest (unless one considers how spectacularly spoiled they are). Particularly susceptible to **IPASCD** are first-time parents; parents who underwent nightmarish, protracted fertility treatments; and Madonna.

treatment /recommendations *

Chances are, your delusion has fostered a difficult, demanding child. Yet, as long as he or she hasn't gone off to college yet, there's still hope. Try the following:

* **INFORM YOUR CHILD THAT YOU MADE A MISTAKE READING HIS IQ** and accidentally doubled the number.

* **NOW CONCEDE TO YOURSELF** that you actually might have done just that.

* **WHILE IT IS TRUE THAT MANY CHILDREN FACE CHALLENGES THAT QUALIFY AS "SPECIAL NEEDS,"** requiring separate classes and government funding, an allergy to kiwifruit is not among them.

* **DOES IT NECESSARILY FOLLOW** that if your child isn't special, you probably aren't special either? Why, yes it does.

* **WHEN PARENTING A PRECOCIOUS CHILD,** it can be hard to remember that in between all the testing and lessons there should be fun as well. Try sending your child to his room for the afternoon or responding to his elaborate arguments with the time-worn phrase "because I said so." He'll hate this, of course, but look how much fun *you're* having!

amateur therapist
DELUSION

DO YOU HAVE AMATEUR THERAPIST DELUSION?

A diagnosis should be based on the following criteria:

* When the cab driver says, "Looks like rain," you tend to respond, "Tell me about that."

* You used to hang out with really cool people. Yet since you began your therapist-like behavior, you've started hanging out with total nut jobs. Surprisingly, it's the same group of people.

* Your flair for dream analysis has been an enjoyable diversion at work, although it didn't go over so well when you explained to your boss that his latest dream, featuring soggy teddy bears, was all about erectile dysfunction.

* Thanks to your advice, friends have left jobs they hated, dared to finally cut their hair, and given in to fantasies of sleeping with escaped convicts. Okay, so maybe that last tip was a bit ill-advised.

* Your analyst has helped you so much, you want to be just like him. But, being a woman, you're having a bit of trouble growing the beard.

background *

Amateur Therapist Delusion (ATD) develops in many patients who mistakenly perceive clinical work to be an easily acquired hobby, like making beer can hats. It is difficult for the layperson to appreciate the years of training that go into learning how to nod in a way that finally stops a grown man from wetting the bed and dreaming of his nose falling off. This is why **ATD** is far more common than, say, **Amateur Surgeon Delusion (ASD)** or **Amateur President of the United States Delusion (APOTUSD)**—although some might say that many presidents themselves have had the latter affliction.

treatment / recommendations *

This delusion is a tough one to get under control. We hear what you're saying and we feel your pain. Process this:

* **FRIENDS TEND TO LEAN ON YOU FOR HELP** because of your skill at asking open-ended questions like "How did that make you feel?" Try instead a close-ended question like "What are you, a pervert?"

* **IF YOU'RE GOING TO BE AN AMATEUR PSYCHOLOGIST,** at least make it profitable. The next time your coffee guy whines to you about his clingy girlfriend, take the tip jar.

* **DEVELOPING ATD** could be a sign that it's time for you to quit therapy altogether. I mean, look at you—strong, healthy, well-balanced, self-actualized, high-functioning . . . Just kidding. Hurry up, or you'll be late for your next appointment.

* **IF YOU'RE GOING TO LISTEN TO PEOPLE DRONE ON ABOUT THEIR MISERABLE LIVES,** they should at least have some visual appeal. Try to cultivate friendships with attractive models and actors. It's amazing, but red-rimmed eyes *can* look hot on the right person.

weekend warrior
DELUSION

DO YOU HAVE WEEKEND WARRIOR DELUSION?

A diagnosis should be based on the following criteria:

✱ You spend every weekend running around a field screaming, "I've got it!" when, in fact, the last time you truly had it was in 1996.

✱ You show more tape than skin.

✱ You realize that when the other members of your amateur soccer team reminisce about college, they're talking about last month.

✱ Hearing that serious backpackers are packing lighter and lighter these days, you head off into the Sierras for the weekend with nothing but a book of matches and some Blistex.

✱ You quit your high-paying job, explaining to your spouse that once you become reigning shot put champ of the entire tri-state region, endorsement checks are bound to coming flying in.

background ✳

In the days when men slaughtered buffalo for a living, making time for manly physical pursuits wasn't such an issue. Now, with the vast majority of men confined indoors during the week, many try to cram a lifetime of hunting and gathering into two exhausting days. Women are less susceptible to this delusion; most are still able to fulfill their need for teamwork, emergency first aid, and mutual consolation in the ladies' room.

treatment/recommendations ✳

Weekend Warrior Delusion can be curbed by acquiring so many injuries that walking feels like an Olympic event. A better solution would be to utilize the following treatment plan:

- ✳ **IT MIGHT BE HELPFUL TO NOTE** that the ability to swim, run, and ride a bike all in one day does not indicate that you are triathlete material. It indicates that you are over the age of five.

- ✳ **SNOWBOARDING IS A DELIGHTFUL SPORT,** yet its culture is perilous for the mature boarder. Anyone over twenty-five should avoid running the half pipe while smoking the whole pipe.

- ✳ **SURE, ROCK CLIMBING "RULES!"** Just not at work. Your boss's habit of practicing his golf swing during budget meetings doesn't give you license to start climbing the filing cabinet.

- ✳ **ASKING YOUR GIRLFRIEND TO PUT ON HER OLD CHEERLEADING UNIFORM** is a standard-issue sex fantasy. Buying her a referee uniform is a clear indication that you still need help.

pets are people too
DELUSION

DO YOU HAVE PETS ARE PEOPLE TOO DELUSION?

Siggy

A diagnosis should be based on the following criteria:

✱ Your dog not only eats better than you do, he eats better than most of France.

✱ You're not bored when your friends discuss their infants because they all sound just like Mr. Pipsy, your guinea pig.

✱ Your supermodel millionaire girlfriend called your pit bull "lame." You just hope the door didn't hit her incredible butt on the way out.

✱ You can't believe it when the other guys at the post office ask if you're lonely since your mother died. *Hello!* You've got more than thirty snakes!

✱ You don't understand why people spend a fortune on down comforters. If they would just sleep with four adorable Huskies—problem solved.

background *

Many people think of their pets as their babies, particularly people without human children. Psychologists actually view this as a normal level of attachment. Yet **Pets Are People Too Delusion (PAPTD)** is diagnosed when the pet owner is actually under the impression that she might have given birth to her iguana. Those suffering from **PAPTD** feel compelled to spend thousands of dollars each year pampering their pets in ways their pets can't appreciate. The powerful pet lobby has blocked all attempts to educate consumers about this expensive delusion. What? You don't think pets could have a lobby? They've got a lobby, all right.

treatment / recommendations *

Like their pets, those with **Pets Are People Too Delusion** respond to simple commands. Here are a few:

* **KING'S GRADUATION FROM OBEDIENCE SCHOOL** is truly an exciting time. Do make him something special for dinner. Don't insist that "Grandma" fly in from Iowa.

* **CONFUSED ABOUT WHY YOUR GUY WON'T MOVE IN WITH YOU?** Try finding new homes for ten of the cats.

* **DON'T BRING JANE TO ANOTHER COCKTAIL PARTY.** She didn't poop on the canapés because she was anxious. She pooped on the canapés because she's a bird.

* **FEEL FREE TO LEAVE FIDO ALL YOUR MONEY.** Just know ahead of time that he's going to blow it all on the bitches.

"i'm a great boss" DELUSION

DO YOU HAVE "I'M A GREAT BOSS" DELUSION?

Siggy

A diagnosis should be based on the following criteria:

* You spontaneously invite several employees over for a barbecue. You're the only one who knows this is a mandatory work event.

* It's been a rough year in your industry, with no bonuses and no raises. That karaoke machine you're setting up in the cafeteria ought to take the sting out of things.

* You pride yourself on your great listening skills. After all, once employees feel as though you really care, they're happy to do it your way.

* Nothing has changed since you were promoted over your peers and made their manager. That constantly bitter look on their faces? Probably just hemorrhoids.

background *

New managers are most susceptible to this affliction, anxious to establish a "family" of colleagues where everyone is "great friends"—just like in television land. Uncomfortable with their authority, they often acquire **"I'm My Kid's Best Friend" Delusion** as well. Thus, everyone wonders why, if we're all equal, only one of us gets to pick the bedtimes and drive the Jaguar.

IN HER MIND, Lauren was the boss she had always wanted to have. So when a consultant was hired to work on company management issues, Lauren assumed she'd be held up as a role model. Instead, her employee feedback report read like a bad review. She was "patronizing and a micromanager," she discovered. Though "full of surface enthusiasm," her staffers should expect any suggestion to "get kicked to the curb before long." Perhaps most devastating was the respondent who simply wrote: "Gives me the willies."

"I don't get it!" Lauren whined to the consultant, "I work so hard to be the kind of boss an employee would love." At that point, the consultant realized that he was dealing with "I'm a Great Boss" Delusion, or IAGBD. He explained to Lauren that she had, in fact, never been a real boss,

vacillating as she did between loving playmate and overinvolved parent. In time, the consultant got Lauren to see that her only job was to give people reasonable pay for reasonable work.

Lauren's new detachment had the desired effect on her employees. "We used to hate her" one employee mused, "Now she's so cool to work for that we'd like her to join us for our weekly happy hour." To the employee's surprise, however, Lauren repeatedly declines the invite. "Now that I'm not trying so hard to bond with my employees, I realize they're kind of annoying," she admits. At the consultant's suggestion, Lauren got a cat and spends her nights expending love where it will be returned. Well, theoretically. "Whiskers is doing great!" she reports. "I just want to see a little more work on the old scratching pole . . ."

treatment/recommendations ✳

"I'm a Great Boss" Delusion is difficult to treat. It is far
more enjoyable to view the workplace as a home away from home
rather than what it is: a Darwinian hell with coffee breaks. Yet those
afflicted who are ready to face reality can try the following:

✳ **USE "MENTOR" AS A VERB** and expect to be mocked.

✳ **LETTING AN EMPLOYEE LEAVE EARLY** to go to a child's school play is
nice. Showing up yourself, wearing an "Uncle Stu" name tag, is creepy.

✳ **SISTERHOOD IS POWERFUL,** but boundaries are still important. Always
borrow tampons from fellow vice presidents.

✳ **AS YOU WALK PAST YOUR FORMER PEERS** having a good time in the break
room, acknowledge to yourself that it's sad to no longer be one of them. Alleviate
your grief by borrowing the corporate jet for a weekend in Bermuda.

did you know?

IN A RECENT SURVEY OF ONE HUNDRED MIDLEVEL CORPORATE
EMPLOYEES when asked what qualities they looked for in an employer,
62 percent said they look for "someone who appreciates my talent and
hard work, and rewards me accordingly," 37 percent said "someone who
has a good work/life balance and encourages employees to take time off,"
and 1 percent said "someone who will stop giving me this crap about how
he can't leave his wife *just* yet."

SLEEP DISORDER:

One of a group of conditions that causes nocturnal disturbance resulting in sleep deprivation

PART V : **sleep disorders**

day gone wrong
INSOMNIA

DO YOU HAVE DAY GONE WRONG INSOMNIA?

Siggy

A diagnosis should be based on the following criteria:

* You lie awake each night agonizing over every tiny mistake, problem, weird conversation, and missed opportunity you had that day.

* In a desperate attempt to correct your failings, you often arise at 2 AM to leave voice mail for friends or send e-mail to colleagues.

* You can't help yourself. You need to talk—now. So your partner is often awakened by your "nightmares": "No! No! Get away from me, Giant Bee Lady! Oh, what? Wow. Was I *dreaming*? That was so real . . . Listen, I'm glad you're up . . ."

* To torture yourself, you often "rewind" your mental tape to relive the exact moment at which your day started falling apart. You convince yourself that if you had only entered the coffee shop two minutes earlier, your soul mate would have been in front of you in line, ordering the exact same double shot mocha to go, and you would have gazed deeply into each other's eyes, and the rest of your life would have been filled with pleasure and devotion.

background *

There is evidence to suggest that **DGWI** is far from a new disorder—cavemen no doubt tossed and turned each night, muttering, "We should have followed that herd west. But no, I had to listen to Miss 'I'm-Sure-There're-Still-Dinosaurs-Out-There'." **DGWI** is actually a mild sleep disorder; those afflicted with *Life* **Gone Wrong Insomnia** are really paralyzed. It is one thing to worry about tomorrow's meeting, it is quite another to spend night after night wondering why you chose the theme from *Caddyshack* for your eighth-grade gymnastics routine.

treatment / recommendations *

Curing any form of insomnia requires both determination and patience. These methods have been known to help sufferers:

* **DON'T JUST LIE IN BED,** living and reliving your difficult day. Get up and read an incredibly boring book. Your roommate's unpublished novel will work nicely.

* **TAKE MILD SLEEP MEDICATION** if it will help, but only for a limited period of time. Be mindful that sleep medication comes in a tiny plastic bottle, not that nice big glass bottle from Russia that you keep in the freezer.

* **"REFOCUSING" TECHNIQUES** can get your mind off daytime worries. Try to recite all of the state flowers, count backward from two hundred, count the moles on your body, remember that you were supposed to make an appointment this week to get that one mole checked, notice that it seems a bit bigger than it did last month, recall that that's one of the signs of malignancy, realize that you might die before ever getting your own talk show, plan who would have been on your show if you were going to live long enough to have one . . .

* **WARM MILK IS OFTEN A COMFORT** for the sleep-deprived. Others swear by warm bodies.

new baby
NARCOLEPSY

DO YOU HAVE NEW BABY NARCOLEPSY?

A diagnosis should be based on the following criteria:

★ You have a new baby.

★ Your baby, like most babies, feels he or she best expresses him or herself through piercing shrieks at all hours of the day and night.

★ During the day, you fall asleep constantly while holding the baby. Fortunately, warm spit-up dribbling onto your neck is a surefire wakeup call.

★ You are constantly reading to the baby in a vain attempt to get him or her to rest. Amazingly, your baby does not find *Pat the Bunny* the snoozer that you do.

background ✶

Narcolepsy is characterized by sudden fits of REM sleep that occur at various times of the day, usually without any warning. Parents of infants are susceptible to this disorder due to the enormous difficulty newborns have in telling time. With a baby screaming uncontrollably at all hours of the day and night, parents have to try to sleep whenever they can. The upside is that parent/child bonding occurs, with parents developing similar feelings of helplessness and a desperate craving for the bottle.

treatment/recommendations *

New Baby Narcolepsy is most easily cured by the child going off to college. In the meantime, these tips might be useful to the chronically sleep-deprived:

* **BE REALLY RICH.** This way you can have around-the-clock nannies to watch junior while you rest in your palatial master bedroom.

* **IT IS INADVISABLE FOR NARCOLEPTICS TO DRIVE.** Hire a chauffeur for the duration of your child's infanthood. If you can't afford this luxury, don't leave the house without a crash helmet.

* **TRY TO NAP WHENEVER THE BABY NAPS** in order to catch up on sleep. Should the baby insist on napping during your favorite soap, poke him or her awake until the next really lame show comes on.

* **IT ISN'T A GOOD IDEA TO LET YOUR FAMILY LIFE INTERFERE WITH WORK.** So when you fall asleep on the conference table and your boss wakes you with, "Baby keeping you up at night?" be sure to respond: "Gosh, no. We've got all that under control. This meeting is just incredibly boring."

embarrassing dreams
ANXIETY DISORDER

DO YOU HAVE EMBARRASSING DREAMS ANXIETY DISORDER?

A diagnosis should be based on these criteria:

* You're afraid to go to sleep at night, because who knows what will be dredged up in your subconscious.

* You used to talk to Barney from the mail room every morning. Then you dreamed that you were his sex slave. Now you hide under your desk when he makes a special delivery.

* Over breakfast, when your mate innocently inquires, "How'd you sleep last night, honey?" you retort defensively, "Listen, I'm not a pervert, okay? So stop grilling me!"

* Your college roommate once found a dream journal you kept and asked why a business major was so into sci-fi pornographic poetry.

background *

Those afflicted with **Embarrassing Dreams Anxiety Disorder** often come from very stable homes and have experienced little or no trauma in their lives. Embarrassing dreams are simply the revenge of the dysfunctional on the functional.

treatment /recommendations ✳

This awkward disorder can make you afraid to go to bed at night.
Get your beauty sleep again by trying the following:

✳ **PEOPLE HAVE A COMPULSION TO SHARE UNUSUAL DREAMS,**
and they're often fun to hear. Nonetheless, choose your audience wisely. Don't
tell your father that you turned him into a bisexual dolphin and then expect
to borrow the car.

✳ **AVOID ANYTHING THAT MIGHT BE FODDER FOR DREAMS:** television,
movies, books, theater, conversations, travel, work, relationships, interactions of any
kind. In fact, you really should go live in one of those sensory deprivation tanks.

✳ **DON'T CONFUSE DREAMS WITH REALITY.** Your local Starbucks may be
filled with slackers, but they are probably out-of-work dot-commers, not CIA hit
men. You'll look like an lunatic sidling up to some schlub with a laptop and
whispering, "There *was* a second gunman, wasn't there?"

✳ **IF YOU CONTINUE TO HAVE PARTICULARLY STRANGE DREAMS,** try to
find the deeper meaning in what appears to be a mishmash of strange, unrelated
images. Soon a clear message will emerge—namely, that you're a big, big freak.

what do your dreams reveal about you?

IF YOU DREAM OF	YOU'RE THINKING ABOUT
Getting lost	A hard decision
Water	Peace
Fire	Fear
Snakes	Penises
Peanuts	Former president Jimmy Carter
Sex	Sex

ADDICTION:

**Behavior involving compulsive
and continued repetition of an activity
despite detrimental consequences**

PART VI

addictions

weird drink
ADDICTION

Siggy

A diagnosis should be based on the following criteria:

✳ You think "chocolate" and "martini" are two words that belong in the same sentence.

✳ You frequently find yourself crowding around others, waiting your turn to drink out of a hose. Yet none of you are children in someone's backyard.

✳ When faced with a perfectly chilled glass of premium vodka, you rush to your spice rack to see what you can add to "give it some zip."

✳ Your favorite drink involves so many frozen treats and decorations floating on top that it resembles the lifeboat scene in *Titanic*.

✳ You head out to some overpriced club because the bartender is known for concocting unique drink specialties—never mind that this is the same kid who almost blew up your high school back in 1994.

background ✳

Although **Weird Drink Addiction** has flourished since the '50s, it has increased recently with the rise in alcoholism awareness. Psychiatrists theorize that individuals alleviate guilt with drinks that involve such complex assemblage they scarcely resemble alcohol at all.

treatment/recommendations ✳

For the first two weeks of treatment, keep a drinking diary when you go out with friends (notes scrawled on a cocktail napkin with lipstick are fine). Note any drinks you order that are brightly colored, bedecked with wacky straws, or that seem to involve several of the basic food groups. These should all be taken as warning signs.

✳ **AS PART OF YOUR NEW REGIMEN, REFUSE TO LOOK AT THE BAR'S SPECIALTY DRINK MENU.** Remind yourself that real drinks don't require funny descriptions; they require bottles.

* **WEIRD DRINK ADDICTS OFTEN SUFFER FROM MIND/BODY DETACHMENT.** A helpful exercise is to put on your most sophisticated evening wear, then stand in front of a full-length mirror. Smile at your reflection and say, "I'd like a gin and tonic, please." Then smile into the mirror and say, "I'd like an Orgasmic Peach Brain Drain, please." Note the disparity between the sophistication of the ensemble and the ludicrous person wearing it.

* **FOR AT LEAST SIX MONTHS, AVOID BARS THAT HAVE FUN NAMES,** trendy exteriors, or attractive young people streaming in and out. Instead, allow yourself to indulge only in "old guy" bars, the kind of establishments where grizzled veterans of real and imaginary wars sip hard liquor through their remaining teeth. Your sexual/romantic prospects will dim, but you'll leave each night inebriated, integrity-filled, and inspired to make an appointment for that yearly dental cleaning.

what does your drink reveal about you?

COSMOPOLITAN:	I'm a trend addict
MIMOSA:	Sun's up! Time to party.
GIN AND TONIC:	Drunkard, yet well bred
WINE COOLER:	Under twenty-one
ROB ROY:	Over fifty
BOURBON, NEAT:	Just keep pouring
AMERICAN BEER:	Whoo-hoo!
IMPORTED BEER:	First bottle—Networking
	Sixth bottle—Whoo-hoo

miracle food
ADDICTION

DO YOU HAVE MIRACLE FOOD ADDICTION?

Siggy

A diagnosis should be based on the following criteria:

✳ You constantly labor under the delusion that some new, previously ignored "magical" food will keep you fit, disease-free, and bursting with health.

✳ First, you were all about carbs, eating six bowls of pasta a day. Then you became the no-carb fanatic, subsisting on bacon-wrapped beefsicles. Surprisingly, all this self-discipline hasn't resulted in any weight loss.

✳ For a mover and shaker such as yourself, energy bars are the way to go. That's why you often eat twenty a day.

✳ There's nothing like a smoothie for a healthy lunch on the go. You can't live without the California Kicker, which is loaded with twelve protein powders plus immune-boosting barnacles scraped off an Alaskan oil tanker.

background *

Miracle Food Addiction was traditionally a female disorder, yet in recent years men have shown they can be just as weird about eating as any teenage girl. Rationalization varies with gender, however. Whereas women confess to "magical thinking" about certain foods, male addicts believe that if one helping is good for you, five would be better. Yet both men and women find their desire to eat rationally thwarted by the government's recent makeover of the basic food group pyramid. Once a reliable method to determine what foods one should consume, the pyramid was recently inverted, regrouped, and then inexplicably reshaped into the profile of Alfred Hitchcock.

treatment/recommendations *

Tired of chasing after the elusive perfect food product? Try swallowing these suggestions:

* **WHEN CONSIDERING A NEW "WONDER" FOOD,** find out which celebrities are scarfing it down. Then, if that isn't enough of a turnoff, consider that you might not be bright enough to be creating your own diet and seek the help of a nutritionist.

* **ORGANIC FOOD IS WELL WORTH THE EXPENSE.** Yet practice some discernment. Be suspicious of "organic" gummy bears from the convenience store, for instance.

* **IT'S TRUE WHAT THEY SAY ABOUT SOY.** When in doubt, eat soy, drink soy, and encourage others to do the same. But keep in mind that naming your first child Soy will not expose you to cancer-fighting agents, only ridicule.

* **BE HONEST WITH YOURSELF.** Some days, you just aren't a "machine" in need of "fuel." Some days you're a depressive in need of chocolate.

HARRY AND JESSICA BOWLES ARE CLASSIC miracle food addicts. Almost every month, one of them comes home from work agog over some new "wonder" diet or "antiaging" food. Well into their thirties and nervous about encroaching middle age, they share a longing to look and feel the same way that they did when they met as college sophomores in Ann Arbor.

"I was in a band then," Harry muses fondly, "Sometimes I'd go weeks eating nothing but frozen burritos."

"If only you'd thawed them first," Jessica adds with a grimace.

The Bowles have long since laid frozen food to rest. Yet strange dietary desires remain. Once they ate nothing but red meat for a month. Then meat became the devil and it was all about combining fruits and grains at four-hour intervals.

Despite their rigorous attention to diet, Harry and Jessica remain a solid ten pounds above their college weight, just like most of their friends. The difference is in attitude; Miracle Food Addiction allows them to feel in control of their health, lending excitement to what might otherwise be a dull, suburban existence. For this reason, they have no interest in therapeutic intervention, even while they acknowledge that their behavior is somewhat delusional. In fact, Harry finds the label rather invigorating.

"I'm an addict?" he responded when a friend confronted him recently. "Cool! I was never an addict back when I was in a band."

reality television show ADDICTION

DO YOU HAVE REALITY TELEVISION SHOW ADDICTION?

A diagnosis should be based on the following criteria:

✶ You watch at least five reality-based shows a week.

✶ In your obsession with the trumped-up reality shown on television, your actual reality—work, relationships, hobbies—has been all but forgotten.

✶ The first thing you say when you meet people is, "Did you see *Naked Stranger Cocktail Party* last night?" This was particularly memorable at that White House reception.

✶ You began watching these shows for ironic enjoyment, but that was three hundred hours ago. Last night, when Byron chose to go windsurfing with Kayla instead of Jade, you found yourself sobbing.

✶ You often wander through your own life pretending to be on a television show. Your family thinks of you as contemplative, but you're just practicing for the freeze-frame.

✶ When your girlfriend dumps you after a year, your first thought is, "What a way to wrap up the first season!"

background *

Like lemmings going to the sea, there is seemingly no end to the number of attractive stupid people willing to humiliate themselves on camera for the slim chance of winning a lot of money or dating a gay telemarketer pretending to be a straight Bill Gates. Due to the proliferation of reality television shows, one can no longer go to the supermarket without seeing a shopper and thinking, "I know that butt from somewhere. Oh yeah, I saw it naked under a waterfall in Tahiti."

Although many have grown weary of the reality craze, others find themselves unable to change the channel. **Reality Television Show Addiction** crops up in those for whom personal reality is a particularly disappointing blend of tedium and irritation. The rest of us, for whom reality is only a petty annoyance, prefer cop dramas.

treatment / recommendations *

It's difficult for true addicts to leave fantasy island, but these tips should have you back to reality in no time:

* **REMIND YOURSELF THAT THESE SHOWS REALLY HAVE NOTHING TO DO WITH REAL LIFE.** In real life, it takes years to find a gorgeous soul mate and acquire a lot of money and fame. In real life, most people never do any of those things. Now don't you feel better?

* **DON'T ATTEMPT TO QUIT COLD TURKEY.** Move over to political talk shows, the methadone of reality television addiction.

* **KEEP A LOG OF HOW MANY REALITY SHOWS YOU WATCH PER WEEK** and rate them in order of your favorites. Each week, eliminate one show from the mix and replace it with a reflective activity (board games, reading, knitting) until your life resembles a homespun Mennonite sea of tranquility. This method is foolproof—especially on paper.

case history

✶ ✶ ✶

Greg: Addicted to Reality

ONE MIGHT THINK that Reality Television Show Addiction hits hardest those with empty lives. Such was not the case with Greg Ames. Greg's schedule was a busy, happy mix of teaching prep school, playing with his young children, and enjoying evenings out with his lovely wife. By all accounts, life was sweet.

Then reality television shows appeared, and Greg's life crumbled. Each night he rushed the children's bedtime stories so he could hit the couch before the first "romantic date" began. At first, he tried to tell himself that this was a harmless diversion, like watching sports. Yet other men looked at him strangely when he'd blurted out, "Talk about games! Could you believe what Marcus said to Alysha when they went dancing without Melanie?"

In the beginning, Greg's wife was a good sport about his new "hobby," but soon grew weary of telling people that Greg couldn't come to the phone because someone was about to be kicked off the Lear jet and sent back to Tacoma. The final straw came when Greg's head-master got himself cast on *America's Sexiest Principals* just so he could remind Greg to come to work in the morning.

"Being a literature teacher, I just kept telling myself that I was in it for the compelling narrative. What a joke! I was in it for the booty." Greg is grateful to Survivors of Reality for his recovery. "I couldn't have done it without this group," he reflects. "Imagine, twelve complete strangers coming together to bare secrets and heal each other, to fight, make up, and move on with our lives . . . Hey, wait a minute. There's a *show* in this! I'm sorry, what were we talking about?"

personal
video recorder
ADDICTION

**DO YOU HAVE PERSONAL
VIDEO RECORDER ADDICTION?**

A diagnosis should be based on the following criteria:

* You originally got TiVo (or a similar device) because, as a discerning television viewer, you wanted total control over your viewing habits.

* Within two weeks, you filled all sixty hours allotted on your recorder and can't believe you didn't spring for the ninety-hour "Power Package."

* Your great consolation when you run out of recording space is the joy you take in eliminating shows from the hard drive. In fact, between recording and canceling, you're far too busy most nights to watch anything.

* Owning a PVR empowers you to the extreme. How extreme? When you heard a major network was looking for a new head of programming, you sent in your resume outlining the details of your astute TiVo decisions.

background *

It used to be we watched what they gave us to watch. Then they gave us a lot more to watch. Now television resembles a vast wasteland of effluvia from which we can choose and reject at will. Personal video recording devices lull people into thinking that they have more control than ever over their televisions. In reality, man is as much a slave to this machine as any other. Man would argue, of course, that this machine is different— this machine offers porn around the clock.

treatment / recommendations *

Are TiVo and its brethren turning you into a crazed vidiot?
Just press play on these helpful hints:

* **TURN OFF THE TELEVISION AND READ A BOOK.** No—we're just kidding.

* **WHILE WE KNOW YOU ENJOY THE CONSTANT, COMFORTING BEEP OF THE RECORDER,** awaken from your reverie long enough to consider that it might be the fire alarm.

* **MONITOR YOUR BEHAVIOR FOR STRANGE THOUGHTS** that sound nonsensical. If you find yourself shrieking to your spouse, "But I have to tape that movie! It's the role I've always wanted to see John Goodman play!"— you know you've gone too far. No one is that passionate about John Goodman except, quite possibly, Mrs. Goodman.

* **ONCE YOU REALIZE THAT IT'S THE TAPING OF SHOWS THAT'S GOT YOU OBSESSED,** rather than the shows themselves, work on transferring this acquisition drive to something a bit more productive. Money makes for a lovely collection and would be sure to draw the admiration of attractive young people.

Rick: Recorder with a Record

OUR PRISONS ARE FILLED with a million stories, all of them sad. Rick Turner's is no exception. Through a prison psychiatrist, Rick finally learned that PVR Addiction was the cause of his downfall and eventual incarceration—a lesson learned too late.

"I loved the recorder when I first bought it" Rick recalled. "The recorder would make suggestions, and they were always good ones. Every day I'd look at the television guide and plot my strategy. At first, I watched all the shows, even if I had to pull an all-nighter. Then it became hard to keep up."

It also became hard for Rick to keep up with his personal life. "My girlfriend got kind of ticked off when I chose to stay home on Saturday night," he admits. "But, come on. She wanted to go salsa dancing. TiVo found a cool spy movie from the '50s. Who knew me better?"

Then, one night, disaster struck. His recorder went on the fritz, first recording hours of unwanted design shows, then erasing all his favorite cop shows.

Rick tried everything, but the machine seemed to have a mind of its own. After months of dominance, Rick couldn't take it. He grabbed a crowbar and smashed his television to bits, causing quite an explosion.

When the police arrived, the machine and its components were so brutally destroyed that they had to rule it a homicide. Rick is serving two to five, but his addiction still haunts him.

"There's one television in the lounge here, and you'd get pummeled if you ever tried to switch the channel. So I close my eyes and fantasize that it's got a recorder, and I'm in charge. I may be in prison, but in my mind? It's *Law and Order*, 24/7."

ebay ADDICTION

A diagnosis should be based on the following criteria:

✱ You're known to all your friends as the "eBay Queen"—or, if you're a male . . . you're still called the "eBay Queen."

✱ You're on such intimate terms with postal employees that you know who's working, who's off, who's doing time for concealed weapons.

✱ Irrationally angry at a seller for how much you had to bid to win, you yearn to leave negative feedback. Finding nothing wrong with the product you instead warn others about his "creepy" handwriting.

✱ You always carry a laptop so you can check your bids whenever you have a spare moment—like waiting your turn to go down the emergency airplane slide.

✱ Everything in your house was purchased on eBay. Granted, everything in your house is mismatched and hideous. Yet you hope never to lose sight of the fact that you won those plastic faux colonial chairs and that huge oil painting of Tina Sinatra. You're a winner!

background *

As a combination auction house and garage sale, eBay taps into two Western obsessions: buying garbage and winning at games. Collectors are particularly susceptible to the addiction. They plan to confine their eBay forays to hunts for china patterns from the 1930s and, in the early stages, enjoy success at finding rare pieces at a bargain price. Yet in no time at all, they turn into hollow-eyed, obsessive addicts, up half the night plotting their auction strategy, gleefully outbidding "some loser in Australia" for seven packets of secondhand underwear.

treatment/recommendations *

If your brain seems to be going once, going twice . . . maybe it's time to get off the auction block. Consider this approach:

* **FIRST AND FOREMOST, YOU CAN'T BUY OR SELL IF YOU DON'T GO ON EBAY.** Perhaps it's time to take a look at all the other things the Internet has to offer that you've been ignoring. For example, online magazines, porn sites, that unopened e-mail entitled "Dad's failing fast, please come home" . . .

* **CAN'T QUIT ENTIRELY?** Focus on slowing down your selling impulse. eBay addicts tend to wander the house, looking for things that they have no interest in but others might want. Look hard at that cute objet d'art that you have little use for and others might find adorable. Is it really yours to sell? Or does it belong to another member of the family? If so, put your sister's baby back down.

* **SHARING IN A SUPPORTIVE ENVIRONMENT** is often the first step to recovery. Consider joining an eBay Anonymous group in your area. Although old habits die hard, try not to be one of the participants shouting out frantic bids for the church folding chairs.

high fidelity
ADDICTION

DO YOU HAVE HIGH FIDELITY ADDICTION?

A diagnosis should be based on the following criteria:

* You buy upward of fifteen CDs a week.

* You go to at least three concerts a week or wish you could.

* Your favorite movies are *High Fidelity*, *8 Mile*, and *Amadeus*. In fact, you enjoy any film where misunderstood music nuts ultimately triumph.

* It's not enough that you have your favorite album in vinyl and CD (and own every song separately, either as a single or cut off a compilation album). You also own all the live recordings of it, except for that one rumored bootleg from Sweden that you can't find. Damn Sweden!

* Your romantic partners have all complained that you cared more about music than you cared about them. Wah, wah, wah, you're sick of hearing it. Wait a minute—that's a cool beat, isn't it? Wah, wah, wah . . .

background *

There have always been music enthusiasts, yet never before in history has one had the opportunity to live one's entire life by sound track. With the ability to have music playing at all times, some aficionados take it to the extreme and feel empty without a constant beat to accompany their every waking move. The greatest sufferers are even happy to have a Michael Bolton ballad stuck in their head. At that point, hospitalization is one's only recourse.

treatment / recommendations *

Are you a hopeless music junkie, constantly jonesing for an aural fix? Try the following:

* **GET A JOB IN A MAINSTREAM CD SHOP** in the worst strip mall in town. When you're exposed day after day to the tripe most people put down money for, you might sour on the whole industry altogether.

* **DATE A DRUMMER.** Enough said.

* **STILL CAN'T SHAKE YOUR ADDICTION?** Confine your social life to other music junkies. Spend hours in passive-aggressive competition over who knows the most about the Mekons. Move into a garage covered in cheap padded soundproofing and littered with amp cords and taco wrappers. This way, you'll live a rich and rewarding life, and the rest of us can get some reading done.

MOOD DISORDERS:

Disorders that create disturbances in mood

IDENTITY DISORDERS:

Disorders that create identity confusion

bipolar neat/messy cycle DISORDER

DO YOU HAVE BIPOLAR NEAT/MESSY CYCLE DISORDER?

A diagnosis should be based on the following criteria:

DURING A NEAT CYCLE YOU:

✶ Buy every container at every store that specializes in containers.

✶ Compulsively line up everything in your apartment: shoes, spices, the cats, and so on.

✶ Get so into the laundry you divide the whites into creams, eggshell whites, and chalk whites.

✶ Don't let anyone wear their shoes in the house (except the people whose socks are even less hygienic).

DURING A MESSY CYCLE YOU:

✶ Have so many piles of crap on the floor that your twelve-foot ceiling shrinks to nine feet.

✶ Can't find anything, including—most troubling—the guinea pig cage.

✶ Get so far behind with the laundry that your clothes are no longer in style.

✶ Don't let anyone in your house. (They might notify the Department of Health.)

background *

Most people are either tidy or sloppy, but those afflicted with **Bipolar Neat/Messy Cycle Disorder (BN/MCD)** vacillate between the two extremes with little memory of how they were before. **BN/MCD** often afflicts adult children of divorce, particularly if joint custody required that they spend half their days in a furniture museum and the other half in a shantytown. Others raised in this manner polarize in a different way, keeping their apartments spotless and their relationships messy.

treatment / recommendations ✶

Tired of jumping from Oscar to Felix so often that you've become your own odd couple? Get off the organizational roller coaster with these helpful hints:

✶ **COGNITIVE WORK CAN BE HELPFUL** to those in the throes of extreme behavior. Instead of aspiring to a flawless home, find a middle ground in which things are a bit unkempt yet eggnog is never found behind the piano in July.

✶ **DURING A NEAT CYCLE,** be sure to do lots of heavy lifting and fast-paced vacuuming. That way, when you revert to spending the day watching videos and wiping barbecue sauce off your chin with your T-shirt, you won't get quite as fat.

✶ **YOU MIGHT WANT TO CONSIDER** one of the vast array of psychotropic medications available to moderate mood swings; they are often hugely effective in evening out neat/messy cycles as well. Afraid that medicine might flatten out your sparkling personality as well? Have no fear. You're weren't that interesting in the first place.

what cycle are you in now?

	NEAT CYCLE	MESSY CYCLE
Favorite food	Fresh organic produce	Pizza crusts from garbage
Favorite outfit	Crisp linen	Underwear, if there's company
Favorite work excuse	"I'm still proofing it."	"I used it for toilet paper."

supermarket acting-out DISORDER

DO YOU HAVE SUPERMARKET ACTING-OUT DISORDER?

A diagnosis can be based on the following criteria:

* You snag so many free samples that the manager asks if you'd like to see a wine list.

* You're always badgering the clerks with impossible requests, asking for rare Indian spices at convenience stores and Wonder bread at upscale markets.

* You think that the express lane rules don't apply to frequent customers like yourself. Never mind that when it comes to buying food, pretty much everyone is a frequent customer.

* You're well known for your great intellect—yet for some reason, when you leave the checkout lane, the tabloid papers are always wrinkled and upside-down in their racks.

background *

During the last economic boom, supermarkets decided that it wasn't enough to sell food, they had to sell a "lifestyle." What was once a simple errand to stock the pantry has become an "experience," complete with cooking demonstrations, gift aisles, and staged events. With shoppers encouraged to stroll aimlessly, eating, drinking, and flirting as they go, acting out behavior is inevitable. In fact, many distracted shoppers leave after several hours without any groceries at all.

treatment/recommendations *

Make a list of everything you need to get at the supermarket and stick to that list. This is an age-old method of saving time and money, and you'll stay focused on the whole purpose of the errand. It might also help to:

* **BE KIND TO OLDER SHOPPERS,** who are often annoyingly slow. Remind yourself that you're buying cereal, not drag racing.

* **BEAR IN MIND** that if others really had time to tell you how to make veal parmesan or what to do with kale, they would have a cooking show.

* **TO SAVE ENERGY,** keep the freezer door closed while you contemplate fourteen varieties of frozen entrées. To save money, just go home and nuke some cardboard for the same taste sensation.

* **IGNORE THE FACT THAT YOU CAN TELL A LOT ABOUT SOMEONE BY WHAT'S IN THEIR CART.** The person next to you at the checkout may not appreciate insights such as, "Recently divorced and living alone with your cats, eh?"

* **REMEMBER:** Sometimes an errand is just an errand. If you insist on jumping heartily into every moment of life, even the little ones, you're bound to be an annoyance to the rest of us.

did you know?

HOSTILE BEHAVIOR IN LARGE SUPERMARKET chains has tripled in recent years, according to *Consumer Behavior* magazine. The report quotes social scientists who attribute this worrisome trend to "our rapidly changing society," "the deterioration of the family," and "the effect of fluorescent lighting on mood." Yet even these factors can't explain the unnerving phenomenon of adult shoppers fighting over the last box of frozen chicken parmesan while armies of small children roam the aisles scavenging snacks like wild jackals.

multitasking attention-deficit
DISORDER

DO YOU HAVE MULTITASKING ATTENTION-DEFICIT DISORDER?

A diagnosis should be based on the following criteria:

* You get an adrenaline rush whenever you start a new project. You wonder if you'll get that same rush when you complete one.

* You have the attention span of a gnat—only they're slightly more focused.

* You think of your car as a great place to have lunch, take conference calls, catch up on your reading, find out who has a top ten hit, get a sunroof tan, and drive—usually all at once.

* Is a friend depressed? No problem. You can do Kegel exercises while mentally rehearsing tomorrow's sales pitch and still appear to be listening.

background *

Multitasking Attention-Deficit Disorder (MADD) is an unfortunate by-product of our technological age. Building the pyramids required real focus, yet now it seems feasible to build a corporation while watching CNN from your treadmill. **MADD** victims value how much one can *say* one is doing rather than how much one actually gets done.

treatment/recommendations *

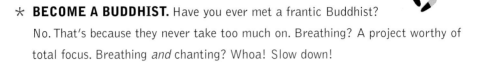

Have you multitasked yourself into the ground? Try these suggestions for a way out (one at a time, please):

* **BECOME A BUDDHIST.** Have you ever met a frantic Buddhist? No. That's because they never take too much on. Breathing? A project worthy of total focus. Breathing *and* chanting? Whoa! Slow down!

* **MADD OFTEN RESULTS FROM THE DEMANDS OF TODAY'S FAST-PACED LIFESTYLE.** You can cut down on your busyness by giving a firm no to every time-consuming request. Surely your brother can get bone marrow from somebody else.

* **ORGANIZING YOUR TIME CAN BE FUN.** Try baking a cake and using the icing to create a master list. Now eat the cake. Nothing will have been accomplished, but who cares? You got cake.

* **THOSE WITH MADD** tend to have an exaggerated view of their own importance. It might be helpful to remember that if you were even remotely important, there's no way you'd be reading this book.

job description
confusion DISORDER

DO YOU HAVE JOB DESCRIPTION CONFUSION DISORDER?

 **A diagnosis should be based on the following criteria:**

✱ When people ask you what you do for a living, you answer with phrases like "manage projects" or "work as a change agent." If they ask more questions, you head for the bathroom.

✱ Because no one at your company is entirely clear on your job function, you're either asked to attend every possible meeting or ignored entirely.

✱ When you attend meetings, your job is to nod thoughtfully and say things like, "Well, it looks like the team is in place for this." You, however, are never on the team.

✱ Year-end evaluations are tricky, since your boss has trouble quantifying your job performance. Usually she just pats you on the shoulder, says, "Thanks for a great year," and gives you a raise.

✱ You always panic during a layoff period at your company, but you're always spared. As no one knows exactly what you do, no one can be sure that you're not essential to operations.

background *

Every company has at least a few employees whose professional demeanor and consistent ability to show up for work every day gives one the impression that they actually *do* something for their paycheck. Sometimes those with **Job Description Confusion Disorder** are lazy charlatans; far more often they are simply people who have moved up the ladder until they've reached a pleasant but empty crawl space.

treatment/recommendations *

Job Description Confusion Disorder is a mild problem and it does have its financial rewards. Yet if you're tired of feeling like just a cog in the wheel, consider the following:

* **TRYING TO FIGURE OUT WHAT YOU'RE SUPPOSED TO BE DOING?** Chances are your title gives few hints, what with its vague wording of "Project Director" or "Vice President, Process Reengineering." Find an acquaintance with the same title at another company, take her out for lunch, and grill her about her specific duties. If she doesn't keep ducking your questions, you might have a viable role model.

* **OFTEN THE HIGHER UP SOMEONE IS IN A COMPANY,** the more gracious he is to the "little people." Since you're probably not busy, spend a morning helping Burt set up chairs in the auditorium. It gives you purpose, and the talk at lunch will be about what a "regular guy" you are.

* **ONE DOWNSIDE TO AN UNCLEAR JOB DESCRIPTION** is that everyone might think you're available and load you up with projects. When you become overwhelmed, try this: inform everyone that you hate to bail on them, but you've been transferred to the El Paso office. Then, when they see you in the halls, let them know that you're "just in town touching base with headquarters." No one will be the wiser.

* **YOU MAY NEVER FIGURE OUT** what you've been hired to do; be sure to have a clear identity in *other* areas of your life to compensate. That way, you can stand up and proudly call yourself a Vegetarian/Pagan/Libertarian Manager of Business Solutions for the Northwest.

too much personality
DISORDER

DO YOU HAVE TOO MUCH PERSONALITY DISORDER?

Siggy

A diagnosis should be based on the following criteria:

* You see yourself as the life of the party. You are alone in this assessment.

* You like to wear fun makeup, fun jewelry, and fun clothes. Oddly enough, you do not work for the circus.

* You always describe your escapades in outsized language, as in, "We worked until ten last night on the year-end fiscal report. O'Brien started snorting Cheetos up his nose. It was supercrazy!"

* While many people have a standard conversation opener, you have limericks.

background *

Those with **Too Much Personality Disorder** were usually extroverted children whose outrageous behavior was viewed as colorful and wrongly encouraged. Many brazen types channel such energy into an acting career. Others choose to make life their stage, a tragedy for the rest of us.

treatment / recommendations *

If your playful persona is actually driving potential playmates away, it might be time to tone things down. Consider the following:

* **TRY TO BE SENSITIVE TO THE GROUP MOOD AT ANY GIVEN EVENT.** After being traumatized by a sudden massive layoff, few coworkers will be enthusiastic about the suggestion that everybody perform a "giant mooning ceremony" in the parking lot.

* **WHEN CHOOSING A MATE,** be sure to pick someone with a knack for keeping your grandiose schemes in check. A suitable partner will gently point out that a wedding at Disneyland is fine, but it is perhaps in questionable taste for the bride and groom to dress like Tweedle Dum and Tweedle Dee.

* **YOU PRIDE YOURSELF ON BRINGING SHY PEOPLE OUT OF THEIR SHELLS.** Consider that they might have built that shell with you in mind.

what your manner reveals about you

CAN'T LOOK PEOPLE IN THE EYE:	Shy or paranoid
LOOK PEOPLE INTENSELY IN THE EYE:	Extroverted or deranged
MAKE FUNNY COMMENTS:	Pleasant company
TELL JOKES YOU GET OFF THE INTERNET:	Annoying as hell
DRESS IN OUTRAGEOUS OUTFITS:	Essentially shallow
LOOK VERY CONSERVATIVE:	Closet freak
SELF-CONFIDENT AND RELAXED:	Annoying as hell

"been there, done that"
DISORDER

DO YOU HAVE "BEEN THERE, DONE THAT" DISORDER?

Siggy

A diagnosis should be based on the following criteria:

✱ No one can ever go to a bar, restaurant, movie, play, or Third World country that you haven't been to first—or so you say.

✱ No one can ever name a prominent townsperson or celebrity without you having a stronger connection to him. If they met him at a fund raiser, you met him at a private party. If they kissed him on the cheek, you've slept with him.

✱ Other people view substance abuse recovery as a perilous, hard-fought battle. You view it as an excuse to tell decadent stories while you sip your Pellegrino.

✱ Your world-weary, pretentious stance relegates you to friendships with no one but Eurotrash and sycophants—in short supply down at the meat-packing plant.

✱ You can say the following sentence aloud, with a straight face: "The watch? It's from my man, P. Diddy."

background *

"Been There, Done That" Disorder (BTDTD) has been around since Eve said to Adam, "Oh please. Don't try to tell me what an apple tastes like." Yet with the advent of easily accessible culture, affordable jet travel, and hyperindulgent parents, it is now possible to have *every* life experience before the age of twenty-one. **BTDTD** emerges in individuals who've done just enough in life to mistakenly believe they've done *everything*. At particular risk for this disorder are interns and personal assistants, who become slaves to experience as well as, simply, slaves.

treatment / recommendations *

Is the glamorous life no longer worth losing your dignity and all your old friends? There is hope for your recovery. Grit your teeth and try the following:

* **RETURN TO THE HOBBIES YOU ENJOYED** before you realized that you were too cool for hobbies. Bowling is an excellent choice, as long as it's not at someone's private alley and written up in *People* the following week.

* **DATE SOMEONE WHO'S NOT** in any business that calls itself "the business."

* **START ADMITTING TO YOURSELF** and others that your long-ago trip to China was three weeks as a tourist, not three years as a resident.

* **START HANGING OUT WITH COMPUTER GEEKS** and scientists just to practice saying, "No, I have no idea what you're talking about. No, I don't know anything about this."

* **GET IN TOUCH WITH YOUR SPIRITUAL SIDE,** which doesn't care about who you know and where you've been; it only cares about where you're going if you keep up this obnoxious behavior: hell, the fiery depths of hell, where Satan awaits with a pitchfork with your name on it. In fact, you're probably already on his list. Try not to brag about it.

uncontrollable channel-surfing DISORDER

DO YOU HAVE UNCONTROLLABLE CHANNEL-SURFING DISORDER?

A diagnosis should be based on the following criteria:

✱ You have upward of three hundred channels on your television and you visit them all, hourly.

✱ You have a constant feeling of dread as you watch one show, assuming you're missing something fantastic on another channel.

✱ You were thrilled when your cable package added the Fly-Fishing Channel. You hate fishing, but it's one more button to push.

✱ Grabbing the remote from your girlfriend, you claim to "just want to check the score." Then you surf through all of the sports channels, movies, news, reruns, and test patterns before returning the clicker so she can try to catch her mother's appearance on *Oprah*.

✱ You own a remote, a universal remote, and a remote remote that lets you change channels on your home TV while you're on a business trip in Asia.

background *

Even feminist scholars concur that there is nothing sexist about it: this is as manly a disease as erectile dysfunction. It is largely confined to heterosexual males who tend to assume that if they click long and hard enough, bare breasts will eventually appear.

did you know?

IN A FIVE-YEAR STUDY conducted by Nelson Media Research, four hundred households were electronically monitored to determine which statements generated the highest across-the-board channel-switching response. Top contenders included:

"in this episode of discovering the wild, we look at the remarkable life cycle of the west african palusi plant . . ."

"this just in: twenty puppies trapped in a raging house fire . . ."

"just what do vern and his grandmother do in their honeymoon hideaway? let's roll that videotape . . ."

"if you're just tuning in, it's pledge week here on public television . . ."

treatment/recommendations *

Although compulsive in nature, **Uncontrollable Channel-Surfing Disorder (UCSD)** is classified with mood disorders due to its tendency to ruin the mood of everyone else in the room. To keep the peace, consider the following:

* **REMEMBER THE LAST TIME YOU READ A GOOD NOVEL?** Following a narrative from beginning to end can be very gratifying (and can put an end to those weird dreams where Lieutenant Briscoe from *Law and Order* suddenly winds up on a rugby field with Larry King).

* **DELUSION NO. 1:** The faster you click, the better the shows get.

* **DELUSION NO. 2:** Your team always seems to make incredible plays while you're up getting another beer or channel surfing. Clearly, you're bad luck for them; keep on clicking and they're bound to win.

* **ONE ARGUMENT IS THAT MEN** only hog the remote because women watch so many "moronic chick shows." Point taken. Please, feel free to switch back and forth between battling robots and *Miss Wet Thong USA*.

inappropriate gift selection DISORDER

DO YOU HAVE INAPPROPRIATE GIFT SELECTION DISORDER?

Siggy

A diagnosis should be based on the following criteria:

* To save time (without scrimping on thoughtfulness), you buy gifts all year round, filling a closet with the basic things that everyone enjoys: a tomato peeler, unisex cologne, a wall-mounted crab that sings "Sea of Love," and much more.

* You feel that if you give from the heart, money is no object—and, in fact, many of your best gifts are found objects from your neighbor's trash or the city dump. You cannot believe the great things that people throw away!

* When your gift is being opened, a phrase you never hear is "Ooh! I've always wanted one of these!" This baffles you. In fact, if you didn't know better, you'd almost think the recipient is pretending not to know what it is.

* People rarely display or wear the gifts you've given them—they say the items are "too precious to risk," despite your reassurances that the Captain & Tennille salt and pepper shakers are unbreakable and that the gold lamé bikini can be dry-cleaned.

background ✳

Inappropriate Gift Selection Disorder (IGSD) affects far more males than females, although mothers of all ages are definitely considered a high-risk group. It is largely hereditary, with both cultural and biological roots. Individuals with **IGSD** seldom receive treatment; a symptom of the disorder is distorted thinking that aids individuals in their denial. Most **IGSD** sufferers think of themselves as inspired gift-givers and even manage to view their rejected presents as signs of "being ahead of the curve."

case history

***

DOUGLAS: Gift-Giver in Recovery

LIKE MANY SUFFERERS OF Inappropriate Gift Selection Disorder (IGSD), **Douglas** Anderson enjoyed giving gifts immensely. In fact, his enjoyment was so great it impeded his ability to see the misery he was inflicting on others.

"I just didn't get it," he admitted after seeking treatment. "Though all the signs were there, when I demanded that my ex give me back the gifts I'd given her over the years, she broke open a bottle of champagne. My teenager told me all he wanted from me for graduation was 'the love between a father and son.' Yet my moment of truth came when I went to a department store days after Christmas and saw everyone I knew at the returns desk. At first I thought it was a coincidence ... then I realized I needed to get help."

Douglas joined a support group that focused on imitating the habits of non-IGSD sufferers until they became second nature. Now he shops weeks before every gift-giving occasion, asks his friends and family what sorts of gifts they might enjoy, and never makes a purchase without first consulting his new girlfriend, a professional personal shopper.

Recovery is not without its disappointments, however. Douglas wistfully recalls such fond memories as the Christmas of 1982, when he gave all his family and friends neon-colored leg warmers. "Good times, good times," he says and sighs. "Well, maybe just for me," he adds, admitting that his girlfriend began sobbing when she opened her gift. "I figured she just had bad taste, but now I understand how sick I really was."

treatment/recommendations ✳

Once you've determined that **IGSD** might be an issue for you, enlist the help of a friend to "retrain your brain" regarding the purchase of gifts. A savvy friend might offer tips like, "What a golfer wants is golf balls, not a golf-themed toilet seat cover."

✳ **LAST-MINUTE SELECTIONS** are usually a disaster for the **IGSD** sufferer. Bear in mind that although a terrific liquor store might be a stone's throw from the party you're attending, a bottle of single malt scotch is not an appropriate bat mitzvah gift.

✳ **AVOID LAST-MINUTE CLOSEOUT SALES,** discount warehouses, and ninety-nine-cent stores. No matter how good a deal you got, your girlfriend will not appreciate a box of plug-in air fresheners, and your grandmother does not want a glow-in-the-dark Frisbee.

✳ **INDIVIDUALS AFFLICTED WITH IGSD ARE OBSESSED** with the notion that a gift should be a big surprise. There are subtle tricks to get around this. When at a shopping mall with a potential gift recipient, one might say, "If you could have three things from this store, what would you pick? Not that I'm going to sneak back here and buy any of them for you. That's just not my style." Carry a notebook and jot down what they covet, while pretending to be working on an article entitled, "Stores I Can't Imagine Stepping Foot in Ever Again."

✳ **IN THAT SAME NOTEBOOK,** record a few simple rules that will steer you *away* from most gift-giving disasters: funny knickknacks aren't funny. Never assume anyone will willingly wear plaid. If you hand someone a book while saying, "I know it's not the kind of thing you usually read," you're handing him a doorstop. When in doubt, give cash; when really in doubt, give a car.

DATING DYSFUNCTION:

A variety of inappropriate or misguided behaviors that result in persistent relationship failure

interesting date planning
DYSFUNCTION

DO YOU HAVE INTERESTING DATE PLANNING DYSFUNCTION?

A diagnosis should be based on the following criteria:

✻ Your constant refrain is "Anyone can go to a nice restaurant or grab a cup of coffee." Anyone but you, that is.

✻ Your idea of an "experienced" date is someone who has already been to the sausage factory.

✻ In your mind, nothing breaks the ice like a midwinter ocean swim.

✻ Your last date landed in the emergency room after one of your escapades. It would make a great story to tell the grandchildren someday. If only she would stop screening her calls.

background ✻

One can blame the rise in **Interesting Date Planning Dysfunction** on any number of economic and sociopolitical factors. Yet, as in many dating dysfunctions, the problem boils down to sex. Before the sexual revolution, couples came up with a variety of odd activities to forestall the evils of intercourse (consider the jitterbug and that whole sharing a soda at the corner drugstore thing). Once sexual congress between unmarried adults became commonplace, dating fell into a simpler routine: meet, drink, fornicate. Yet since the emergence of the AIDS epidemic, people are once again slowing down the courtship rituals and getting to know each other through a wonderful variety of shared experiences. **IDPD** emerges in those who are slow to realize that "wonderful variety" includes things like trips to Belize and walks on the beach, not front row seats at the monster truck rally.

treatment/recommendations *

Interesting Date Planning Dysfunction can be treated rather easily if the sufferer is motivated to change. Yet the following tactics must be employed immediately or backsliding is inevitable:

* **BEFORE YOU PROPOSE A DATING ACTIVITY,** ask yourself, "Do I want to appear exciting and fun? Do I want to show off my knowledge of art galleries specializing in feminist collage?" Remind yourself that these are not the same thing.

* **CONSIDER THE FIRST-DATE UNIFORM.** It should be attractive, yet not too forward. Under no circumstances should it involve a trip to the costume shop.

* **CREATE A MAP OF YOUR AREA** and put pins everywhere you've dragged a new date. If more than three of those pins reside in neighboring states, put yourself under house arrest until the compulsion to combine travel and dating subsides.

* **ARE YOU INCREDIBLY PHYSICALLY ATTRACTIVE?** Relax. If you look like a cast member on the WB, you'll impress your date plenty just by showing up—and being willing to linger on the porch in case the ex drives by.

* **IF BEAUTY, WIT, AND CHARM EVADE YOU,** you're more likely to try the "weird field trip" date. Just know enough to jump ship if you're having a lousy time (although you might want to wait for the harbor cruise ship to dock). At this juncture, your only hope is to fall back on that old standard: getting the date back to your place. A clever outing might not get you anywhere, but a bottle of tequila and lots of compliments might just get you everywhere.

what does your choice of plans reveal about you?

A nice dinner out says	Let's enjoy the finer things in life.
An action movie says	Let's enjoy watching stuff blow up.
Mini golf says	I have a sense of artificial fun.
Playing pool says	I think I'm pretty cool.
Playing poker says	I have a gambling problem.
Meeting my folks says	This relationship has hit a new level.
Meeting my wise old ethnic grandma says	We're characters in some sappy movie.
Meeting early for coffee says	I want to take this slow.
Meeting late for drinks says	To hell with slow.

premature
relationship
DYSFUNCTION

DO YOU HAVE PREMATURE RELATIONSHIP DYSFUNCTION?

Siggy

A diagnosis should be based on the following criteria:

* You learn that an upcoming blind date owns a restaurant and immediately take "food" out of your monthly budget.

* When a first date fails to result in a second one, you call the person screaming, "I can't believe you're dumping me like this!"

* Anyone who agrees to see you twice winds up at your folks' house, looking at family photos while listening to anecdote after anecdote about your precious childhood.

* While many people have sex on the third date, you usually get married.

background *

Premature Relationship Dysfunction (PRD) arises in both men and women, but for different reasons. In women, **PRD** results when guilt over sex causes them to turn every fling into a more legitimate romance. Men tend to suffer from **PRD** when faced with an incredibly beautiful woman. They imagine the house, the dog, the kids, the growing old together, all while the object of their affection is saying, "Is your name Jim or Tim?"

treatment / recommendations ✳

Cognitive therapy can effectively treat those inclined to cry
"soul mate" too soon. Wipe that dreamy expression off your face
and try the following:

✳ **GOOD FRIENDS CAN ALWAYS PROVIDE A ROMANCE REALITY
CHECK.** When they gently suggest that you slow things down with someone
whose last job was making license plates, maybe they're not just jealous of
your newfound happiness.

✳ **PERHAPS YOU'VE BEEN LUCKY** enough to find a guy who loves his work,
gets along with your mother, and wants to have kids. Not so fast, sister. Until you
hear him say, "Those supermodels could really use some meat on their bones,"
don't sign on the dotted line.

✳ **BEAR IN MIND** that you really can't know if someone is right for you in just a
few months. Be sure you've dated him or her long enough to run an FBI check.

top five ways to ensure they'll never call back

5. Tell your blind date on the phone, "You have such a motherly/
fatherly voice."
4. Invite him over for an evening of salad, light beer, and *Terms
of Endearment* on the Oxygen network.
3. When you meet her mother, throw out your arms
and shriek, "Mom!"
2. When she buys you an extravagant present on
your birthday, say, "How sweet! But we've got to
start saving for our retirement, don't we?"
1. Show him a picture of your hairy aunt Lucille and
say, "Look, honey! This will be *me* in twenty years."

gaydar
DYSFUNCTION

DO YOU HAVE GAYDAR DYSFUNCTION?

A diagnosis should be based on the following criteria:

✱ Your coworker's love of Mae West must mean he's a "breast man."

✱ You think it's sweet that your boyfriend wants to wait a while longer because "what we have is more special than sex."

✱ You and your prep school roommate make out a lot. You believe him when he claims it's a seventy-year-old hazing tradition.

✱ There's a bar in your neighborhood called Rear Drive and you think it's a race-car driver's hangout.

background ✱

Gaydar Dysfunction is a learning disability that manifests itself in auditory and visual processing problems. Those with acute gaydar can spot a homosexual anywhere, even at his wedding to your sister. With faulty gaydar, however, sexual orientation signifiers are missed, and one can't see the florist through the trees.

The flurry of television shows and movies depicting gay people has sharpened the gaydar of most Americans. Yet there will always be those men who, for example, insist Brad Pitt is gay. One could argue that delusions like this are based less on faulty gaydar than on the desire to elevate a community forced to embrace Liberace, George Michael, and quite possibly, Winnie-the-Pooh.

treatment/recommendations ✴

Those with **Gaydar Dysfunction** will never become astute observers of sexual orientation, and might still waste precious years pining after someone who would rather go through junior high all over again than sleep with the opposite sex. Yet dating disasters can be avoided with the following techniques:

FOR WOMEN

✳ **GO TO A LARGE NIGHTCLUB** filled with stylish men and practice spotting the straight guys. If he's mangling a beer can, he's your man. (Well, probably not, but at least he'd like to be.)

✳ **WHEN CONVERSING WITH SEXUALLY AMBIGUOUS ARTIST TYPES,** learn to spot telling actions. If he sneaks a glance at your chest, you're in. If he sneaks a glance at your shoes, move on.

FOR MEN

✳ **MEN LOVE TO DATE WOMEN WHO WORK OUT REGULARLY,** yet choice of sport is key. If she out-lifts you by a hundred pounds and worships the LPGA . . . hello, Melissa Etheridge.

✳ **TO COMPLICATE THE ISSUE,** many lesbians resemble standard-issue "hot chicks" and have slept with a man on occasion. Just be sure to get a three-way in before she dumps you.

THROUGHOUT HER TWENTIES, Dana Emerson had no trouble spotting the gay guys. And why should she? The self-proclaimed "fag hag of Southern Oregon" had plenty of men in her life and they all loved other men. Occasional crushes on her gay friends were an uncomfortable by-product, but Dana's attitude was "at least I get to hang around handsome, charming men who think I'm fabulous."

Yet as the years went by, Dana realized that her life was missing that certain something. Her friend Carl helped define it for her: "Honey, you need to get laid." The problem was, by this time Dana had developed an environmentally induced case of Gaydar Dysfunction. It wasn't that she couldn't spot a gay man. It was that *all* men started seeming gay to her. Years of living *Will & Grace*-style had weakened her sexual orientation signifiers. She'd see a pair of stylish shoes and think, "Gay." Her date would get choked up when he talked about his mother's death and she'd think, "Gay."

Needless to say, this did not endear her to the heterosexual men she encountered. They soon tired of her weird questions, such as always asking if they were fans of Liza Minnelli or *Queer as Folk*. "I'd spend half the night defending my sexuality," one guy complained. "By midnight she had me half convinced that I was in love with my Tae Kwan Do instructor."

When she could bear it no longer (and no one could bear her), Dana joined a support group for Gaydar Dysfunction. There she met a sweet guy named Alex who was tired of going to his ex-girlfriends' commitment ceremonies. In no time at all, they formed a commitment of their own.

"i can get that hottie" DYSFUNCTION

DO YOU HAVE "I CAN GET THAT HOTTIE" DYSFUNCTION?

A diagnosis should be based on the following criteria:

✳ You can sense when a hot girl is giving you the eye. Sometimes it's in a club, sometimes on the street, sometimes she's on a billboard.

✳ That new guy in school is gorgeous. Other girls seek his attention with short skirts and low-cut tops, but you're armed with *really* funny stories about band camp.

✳ You're so fixated on a girl being your "exact physical type" that it never occurs to you to wonder if her exact physical type is a scrawny, pimply faced teenager who spends ten hours a day hunched over his Game Boy.

background ✳

"I Can Get That Hottie" Dysfunction is a widespread social phenomenon manufactured by Hollywood. Moviegoers have been brainwashed by decades of romantic comedies in which women throw over handsome boyfriends for guys whose chief charms are stalking and making scenes in public. Bear in mind that these are all merely staged fantasies written by guys trying to get a crack at Julia Roberts.

treatment/recommendations *

It's a sign of healthy self-esteem to try to date out of your league. But if you're in Little League and aiming for the Olympics, you might benefit from the following:

* **PROXIMITY NEVER HURTS.** For instance, an unusually high number of models date their favorite photographers. This proves that while familiarity may breed contempt, it also breeds opportunity.

* **ARE YOU WASTING YOUR TIME CHASING A DREAM?** Sometimes your choice of environment can tip you off. The next time you go to a party, look around the room and find the least attractive person there. If it's you, you're at the wrong party.

* **WHEN TRYING TO WIN OVER A BEAUTY,** consider what qualities you bring to the relationship. If he offers looks, charm, and style, you should not assume that "nice elbows" and "knows lots about John Cleese" will get you very far. Yet if you can add to your list "worth twelve million dollars since my company went public," you just might have yourself a date.

reprogramming the hottie

SOMETIMES YOU CAN GET THAT HOTTIE. Try the following:

Reverse Psychology: "I've dated plenty better looking than you. In fact, I wouldn't go out with you if you begged me. Try it! Go ahead and beg, you ugly mongrel!"

Dr. Phil: "You know why you won't go out with me? Plain and simple fear. Tell me, why do you hold on to that fear? That fear is a jack rabbit with nowhere to go but into a dark hole. You see what I'm saying?"

Cognitive Restructuring: "What's the worst thing that could happen if you went out with me? An evening with a bland-looking dullard? So what. Ever spend a night combing head lice out of your hair? That was worse, wasn't it?"

about the author *

ANDREA CORNELL SARVADY, ignoring her own theory that "the unexamined life is probably pretty darn pleasant," has both been in therapy and practiced therapy on others after receiving a master's in counseling from the University of San Francisco. She has written articles for the *San Francisco Bay Guardian, Pegasus,* the Atlanta *Journal-Constitution* and *Atlanta Woman* magazine, among other publications. After working with children and their families from San Francisco to New York (well, San Francisco and New York), she finds herself giving unwelcome advice in Atlanta, Georgia, where she lives with her husband and an alarming number of young daughters.

about the illustrator *

After studying at Parsons School of Design in both New York and Paris, **ROBIN ZINGONE** fueled her creativity through extensive overseas travel. These days, she's at work on a wide range of design jobs, from illustration for Mattel's Barbie to beer glasses for Anheuser-Busch, a mural for QVC, and scarf designs for Visa. She designed and built her own pamoramic house in rural Connecticut and recently launched her own line of hand-painted pottery. Robin lives with her husband, Peter, and an extended family that includes three dogs and two cats.